INCOGNITO EXPLORERS

UNVEILING HIDDEN HORIZONS

REVELATIONS IN THE SOUL OF ITALY

Jay Chandarana

Copyright © 2024 Jay M Chandarana

Stay connected beyond the pages – join the journey on social media

YouTube: https://www.youtube.com/@incognitodestinations
Instagram: https://www.instagram.com/incognitodestinations
Amazon Catalog: https://amazon.com/author/jaychandarana
Apple books: https://books.apple.com/us/book/revelations-in-the-soul-of-italy/id6479964311?ls=1

TABLE OF CONTENTS

Welcome to Italy: Where dreams and history collide

Echoes of Italy: A Prelude to Timeless Beauty

Italy, often referred to as Italia, stands at the crossroads where dreams and history intertwine in a captivating dance. The very essence of this enchanting country is a seamless blend of ancient legacies and contemporary allure. Its cobblestone streets echo with the footsteps of poets, artists and philosophers who have left an indelible mark on the world. From the grandeur of the Colosseum in Rome to the serene canals of Venice, Italy's landmarks are living chapters in the unfolding saga of human civilization.

Each corner of this timeless land whispers tales of triumphs, defeats and the enduring pursuit of beauty. As you traverse the landscapes of Italy, you'll find yourself immersed in a tapestry woven from the threads of diverse cultures and profound history. The architecture tells stories of bygone eras, with medieval castles perched on hilltops and Renaissance palaces gracing city squares. The vibrant traditions, celebrated through lively festivals and rituals, add a colourful layer to the narrative. Italy's charm lies not only in its historical grandeur but also in the palpable passion of its people, who take pride in preserving their heritage while embracing the modern world. In Italy, dreams take flight against a backdrop of ancient stones, creating a harmonious symphony that resonates through the ages.

Italy's past: Elegance woven through centuries

Embarking on the journey through Italy is like stepping into a living tapestry where the threads of history weave a tale of unparalleled elegance. The past, preserved in cobblestone streets and architectural wonders, is an integral part of the traveller's odyssey. From the grandeur of the Colosseum in Rome to the intimate charm of Tuscan hamlets, every corner whispers stories of a bygone era. In this travel guide, I invite you to explore Italy's past, where the Renaissance not only transformed art and culture but also shaped the very essence of this captivating nation.

As we traverse the landscapes of Tellaro, Castelluccio, Savoca and beyond, each destination unveils a unique chapter in Italy's rich history. The allure of Italy lies not just in its picturesque vistas but in the narratives that echo through time. This guide offers a curated journey through the elegance of Italy's past, inviting you to witness the architectural wonders, artistic masterpieces and cultural traditions that have stood the test of centuries. Get ready to immerse yourself in the elegance woven through Italy's history, where each step is a discovery and each destination reveals a layer of the country's timeless charm.

Italia's traditions: A melody across time

This travel guide orchestrates a journey through the vibrant traditions that echo through the ages, each destination harmonizing with the cultural melody of the country. From the captivating rituals of Savoca to the culinary crescendos of Burano, readers are invited to immerse themselves in a tapestry of festivities, art and local customs. The guide acts as a conductor, leading explorers through the rhythmic celebrations of Varenna, the historic narratives of Pitigliano and the timeless elegance of Ravello. As travellers traverse Italy, they'll witness a living symphony where the past resonates in every tradition, creating a sensory expeirence that amplifies the cultural allure. Whether it's the colourful processions or the intimate tales of each destination, this guide endeavours to capture the enduring spirit of Italy's traditions, inviting readers to dance to the melodious cadence of the country's cultural symphony.

Iconic vistas: Italia's majestic tapestry of famous landmarks

Embarking on the Italian odyssey reveals a majestic tapestry of famous landmarks that stand as timeless witnesses to the country's historical grandeur. From the Colosseum's formidable silhouette in Rome to the leaning elegance of the Tower of Pisa, each landmark narrates a chapter in Italy's architectural and cultural legacy. This travel guide meticulously curates a visual feast of iconic vistas, inviting readers to marvel at the artistry of Florence's Duomo, lose themselves in the intricate labyrinth of Venice's Grand Canal and bask in the opulent splendour of the Vatican City. As we explore these renowned landmarks, the guide aims to be more than a mere map; it strives to be a companion, enriching the traveller's journey with the stories, anecdotes and cultural significance embedded in each stone and sculpture.

Italy's majestic landmarks not only epitomize architectural brilliance but also serve as gateways to the soul of the country. The guide unfolds the narrative behind each landmark – the historical triumphs, the artistic revolutions and the cultural significance that breathes life into the stones. Whether it's the panoramic views from the Amalfi Coast or the intricate details of Milan's Cathedral, this guide transforms the exploration of famous landmarks into a captivating sojourn, where each vista becomes a brushstroke in the vivid canvas of Italy's cultural and historical panorama.

Italy's geographical symphony: Unveiling the mosaic of distinctive regions

This travel guide takes the reader on a melodic sojourn, unveiling the distinctive cadences of each region. From the sun-soaked landscapes of Sicily to the Alpine elegance of the Dolomites, navigating through the rolling hills of Tuscany, the azure coasts of the Amalfi, the vibrant urban pulse of Milan and Rome, the cultural richness of Emilia-Romagna and the sun-kissed fields of Umbria, Italy's geographical composition is a harmonious mosaic. Each region is a chapter in the narrative, revealing its unique cultural heritage, culinary traditions and natural wonders. As readers traverse the geographical symphony of Italy, the guide seeks to provide not just directions but a serenade that captures the essence of each region, inviting them to partake in the rhythm of this multifaceted and enchanting land.

Gastronomic overture: Italia's culinary symphony unveiled

Stepping into Italy is akin to entering a culinary crescendo, where each region composes its own flavourful movement in the symphony of Italian gastronomy. From the truffle-infused delicacies to the citrus-infused flavours of Sicily, the guide unfolds as a gastronomic maestro, inviting travellers to partake in the sensory delights that define each region.

Beyond a mere guidebook, it endeavours to be a companion on a culinary journey, revealing not only the renowned dishes but also the hidden gems, local markets and family-run trattorias that contribute to Italy's unparalleled culinary legacy. As readers traverse this culinary symphony, the guide aims to evoke not just the taste of Italy but the essence of a nation that truly savours life through its delectable creations.

Wanderer's wisps: Navigating Italia's tapestry with grace

Embarking on a journey to Italy is like stepping into a timeless masterpiece, where every cobblestone street, ancient ruin and Renaissance masterpiece tells a story of unparalleled beauty and cultural richness. From the vibrant streets of Rome to the romantic canals of Venice and the sun-kissed shores of the Amalfi Coast, Italy beckons travellers with its captivating blend of history, art, cuisine and natural landscapes. As you prepare for your adventure, it's essential to arm yourself with insider knowledge and practical tips to navigate the wonders of this enchanting country with ease and confidence. Whether you're a first-time visitor or a seasoned explorer, let these travel tips serve as your compass, guiding you through the diverse tapestry of Italy's iconic landmarks, hidden gems, culinary delights and local traditions. Get ready to immerse yourself in the unparalleled charm and allure of Italy, where every moment promises a new discovery and unforgettable experience.

In Italy, the seasons generally align with those of the Northern Hemisphere, with spring lasting from March to May, summer from June to August, autumn from September to November and winter from December to February. Spring brings blooming flowers, mild temperatures and lively festivals, making it an ideal time for outdoor exploration. Summer sees peak tourism, with warm weather perfect for beach vacations and al fresco dining. Autumn offers cooler temperatures, vibrant foliage and harvest festivals celebrating Italy's culinary bounty. Winter brings cooler weather and fewer crowds, ideal for exploring historic sites and enjoying winter sports in the Alps.

When planning your travels in Italy, it's essential to consider the seasonal variations that each region experiences. For example, while summer is perfect for coastal destinations like Cinque Terre and Sorrento, it may be sweltering in cities like Rome and Florence. Likewise, winter offers excellent skiing opportunities in the Alps but may bring colder temperatures and shorter daylight hours elsewhere. To make the most of your trip, research seasonal events, pack accordingly for the weather and consider visiting popular attractions during off-peak times to avoid crowds. Additionally, booking accommodations and transportation in advance can help secure the best deals and ensure a smoother travel experience during peak seasons.

Savour the slow pace

Embrace the Italian way of life by appreciating the art of 'dolce far niente' – the sweetness of doing nothing. Enjoy leisurely meals, take a stroll through charming streets and let each moment unfold at its own pace.

Learn a few Italian phrases
While many Italians speak English, making an effort to learn a few basic phrases in Italian can go a long way. Locals appreciate the gesture and it adds a personal touch to your interactions.

Explore beyond tourist hotspots

Italy is full of hidden gems. Venture beyond the well-known attractions to discover the authentic charm of smaller towns, local markets and lesser-known historical sites.

Dress stylishly and modestly

Italians are known for their fashion sense. Consider dressing smartly, especially when visiting churches and upscale restaurants. Additionally, modest attire is appreciated in religious sites.

Master the art of aperitivo

Join the locals in the early evening ritual of aperitivo. Enjoy a pre-dinner drink accompanied by light snacks. It's a great way to unwind and socialize.

Use public transportation

Italy has an extensive and efficient public transportation system. Consider using trains and buses to travel between cities and regions. It's a scenic and convenient way to explore the country.

Be mindful of pickpockets

Like any popular tourist destination, be cautious of pickpockets, especially in crowded places. Keep an eye on your belongings and use anti-theft measures such as money belts.

Try local cuisine

Italy is a gastronomic paradise. Don't miss the opportunity to try regional specialties. Venture beyond pizza and pasta to discover the diverse and delicious Italian culinary landscape.

Adapt to siesta time

Many businesses, especially in smaller towns, observe a siesta period in the afternoon. Plan accordingly, as some shops and restaurants may close during this time.

Respect local customs and traditions

Italy has a rich cultural heritage. Respect local customs, particularly in religious sites. Be mindful of quiet hours during riposo (afternoon rest) and participate in local traditions when appropriate.

Vipiteno: Alpine elegance in every vista

Jay Chandarana

Alpine echoes: A prelude to Vipiteno's enchanted peaks

Nestled amid the enchanting Alpine landscapes of northern Italy, Vipiteno sits approximately 80 kilometres north of Bolzano, the provincial capital and emerges as a storybook town, inviting travellers into a world where medieval charm harmonizes with breath-taking mountain vistas. Set against the backdrop of the South Tyrolean Alps, Vipiteno, also known as Sterzing in German, is a captivating blend of history, culture and natural beauty. Vipiteno's altitude of 948 meters above sea level makes it an ideal destination for outdoor activities such as hiking, skiing and mountain biking. As you approach this Alpine jewel, the striking sight of pastel-hued buildings framed by snow-capped peaks welcomes you, creating a picturesque scene that seems straight out of a fairy tale.

Founded in the Middle Ages as a vital trading hub, Vipiteno boasts a rich heritage that unfolds through its well-preserved medieval architecture, cobbled streets and historic landmarks. The town's strategic location on ancient trade routes contributed to its economic prosperity, a legacy evident in the elaborate frescoes that adorn centuries-old facades. Today, Vipiteno beckons travellers with its warm Tyrolean hospitality, inviting them to wander through its quaint squares, explore artisanal boutiques and relish the flavours of Alpine cuisine. Whether you're drawn to the cultural allure of the town or the allure of the surrounding peaks, Vipiteno promises an immersive experience where the past seamlessly intertwines with the present in the heart of the Italian Alps.

Prepare to immerse yourself in a world where history meets natural beauty, as we explore the rich cultural heritage and hidden gems of this enchanting mountain town.

Heritage heights: Vipiteno's timeless echoes

Vipiteno, with its roots firmly grounded in medieval history, stands as a testament to the enduring legacy of a bygone era. Dating back to the 14th century, the town's historical significance is deeply intertwined with its strategic location along ancient trade routes, contributing to its role as a bustling mercantile centre during the Middle Ages. As a pivotal hub for commerce and cultural exchange, Vipiteno thrived as a trading post where merchants from diverse regions converged, leaving an indelible mark on the town's cultural tapestry.

The architectural heritage of Vipiteno reflects its historical prominence, showcasing a remarkable collection of well-preserved medieval structures. The Zwölferturm, a towering twelve-sided tower dating back to the 15th century, serves as a tangible reminder of the town's medieval fortifications. The town's main square, Piazza del Mercato (Marktplatz), is surrounded by centuries-old buildings adorned with vibrant frescoes, each mural narrating a chapter of Vipiteno's storied past. The gothic-style Zwölferturm and the striking town hall, with its elegant clock tower, further emphasize Vipiteno's role as a medieval trading and administrative centre. Exploring the winding alleys and historic landmarks of Vipiteno provides a captivating journey through time, offering a glimpse into the town's historical significance and the dynamic cultural exchange that shaped its identity.

Mountain melodies: Vipiteno's symphony of local culture

Vipiteno, nestled within the scenic embrace of the South Tyrolean Alps, is not only a haven for natural beauty but also a reservoir of rich local culture that resonates through its traditions, arts and warm Tyrolean hospitality. The town's cultural identity is deeply rooted in its Alpine heritage and this influence is prominently displayed in the unique

blend of German and Italian traditions that characterize daily life. From the moment you step onto the cobblestone streets, you'll sense the pride the locals take in preserving their distinct cultural heritage, creating an atmosphere where tradition seamlessly intertwines with modernity.

One of the vibrant aspects of Vipiteno's local culture is its dedication to traditional craftsmanship. Artisan workshops line the narrow alleys, where skilled hands fashion intricate wood carvings, detailed ceramics and other handmade crafts. Visitors have the opportunity to witness the creation of these authentic pieces and even acquire them as souvenirs, each item embodying the town's artistic legacy. The commitment to preserving these age-old crafts serves not only as an economic endeavour but also as a means of passing down cultural stories and techniques from one generation to the next.

Peaks of prestige: Exploring Vipiteno's notable landmarks

Vipiteno, a picturesque town nestled in the heart of the Italian Alps, unfolds as a tapestry of historical charm and breath-taking landscapes. Each cobblestone street and historic square is adorned with landmarks that tell the story of Vipiteno's rich heritage. From medieval fortifications to vibrant marketplaces, the town invites visitors to explore its architectural treasures and natural wonders. Join us on a journey through the landmarks and points of interest in Vipiteno, where every corner unveils a piece of the town's fascinating history and Alpine allure.

The Raccolta di presepi

Discover the artistry of the Nativity scene collection, housed in the Civic Museum of Vipiteno. This unique exhibition showcases an extensive array of nativity scenes, reflecting various styles and cultural influences. From traditional to contemporary interpretations, the collection provides insight into the diverse ways in which artists have depicted the nativity throughout the centuries.

Chiesa di San Michele

The Chiesa di San Michele, or Church of St. Michael, is a masterpiece of Gothic architecture that graces Vipiteno's main square. Built in the 14th century, the church boasts a stunning facade adorned with intricate sculptures and a prominent bell tower. The interior features awe-inspiring frescoes and a collection of religious artifacts, offering a glimpse into the spiritual and artistic heritage of Vipiteno.

La Casa delle erbe

Step into the medieval charm of La Casa delle erbe, a historic building that once served as the town's pharmacy. Adorned with frescoes and intricate architectural details, the house reflects the prosperous history of Vipiteno as a centre of trade and commerce. Today, it houses a museum that takes visitors on a journey through the evolution of pharmaceutical practices and herbal remedies.

Torre delle dodici

Dominating the skyline of Vipiteno, the Torre delle dodici, or Tower of the twelve, stands as a symbol of the town's medieval past. Originally part of the town's fortifications, the tower dates back to the 15th century. Visitors can ascend its sturdy stone steps to reach the top, where panoramic views of Vipiteno and the surrounding Alpine scenery reward those who venture to its summit.

The Sterzing Christmas market

Experience the magic of the Sterzing Christmas Market, a winter wonderland that transforms Vipiteno into a festive spectacle. The market, held in the historic town centre, features wooden stalls adorned with twinkling lights, offering handmade crafts, local treats and seasonal delights. The aroma of mulled wine and the sounds of traditional Christmas carols create a magical ambiance, making the Sterzing Christmas Market a cherished annual tradition.

Mineralienmuseum

Unearth the geological wonders of the region at the mining museum, a treasure trove of minerals and crystals. Housed in a historic building, the museum showcases the rich mineral diversity found in the Alps. Visitors can marvel at sparkling specimens, learn about the mining history of the area and gain insights into the fascinating world beneath the surface of Vipiteno's mountainous surroundings.

Il Ponte di San Michele

Crossing the gentle waters of the Eisack River, Il Ponte di San Michele, or Saint Michael's bridge, is a charming pedestrian bridge that connects different parts of Vipiteno. The bridge offers delightful views of the town, the river and the surrounding Alpine landscape. Stroll across its arches, taking in the scenic beauty that makes Vipiteno a picturesque gem in the heart of the Alps.

Jay Chandarana

Piazza municipio

At the heart of Vipiteno, the, Piazza municipio or Town Hall square, serves as a vibrant hub surrounded by colourful buildings and lively cafes. The Gothic-style Town Hall,

with its striking clock tower, anchors the square and adds a touch of architectural splendour. The square is a gathering place for locals and visitors alike, offering a charming setting to enjoy the Alpine ambiance and indulge in the town's cultural richness.

Embark on a journey through Vipiteno's landmarks and points of interest, where each step unveils a chapter of the town's captivating history, artistic heritage and Alpine allure.

Savouring the peaks: Culinary delights in Vipiteno's Alpine retreat

Vipiteno, nestled in the heart of the Alpine region, offers not only breath-taking landscapes but also a rich culinary tapestry that reflects the town's cultural heritage. From hearty mountain fare to sweet indulgences, the local gastronomy of Vipiteno invites visitors to savour the flavours of the Alps. Join me on a gastronomic journey through the charming streets of Vipiteno, where each bite is a celebration of Alpine tradition, local craftsmanship and the artistry of Italian cuisine.

Speck dell'alto Adige

Indulge in the distinctive flavours of Speck dell'alto Adige, a traditional cured and smoked ham that holds a special place in Vipiteno's culinary heritage. The meat is seasoned with a blend of Alpine herbs and spices, then slowly smoked to perfection. Sliced thin and enjoyed as an appetizer or part of a charcuterie board, Alto Adige Speck encapsulates the savoury essence of the Alpine region.

Strudel alto Adige

Embrace the iconic Strudel alto Adige, a delectable apple pastry that showcases the region's apple orchards. Thin layers of dough encase a filling of locally grown apples, nuts and spices, creating a harmonious blend of sweetness and warmth. Served with a dusting of powdered sugar, Strudel Alto Adige is a timeless dessert that pays homage to the bounty of the Alpine landscape.

Kaiserschmarrn

Satisfy your sweet tooth with Kaiserschmarrn, a fluffy and caramelized pancake that has become a beloved dessert in Vipiteno. The pancake is torn into pieces while cooking, creating a delightful mix of textures. Often served with powdered sugar and fruit compote, Kaiserschmarrn is a decadent treat that captures the essence of Alpine indulgence.

Canederli

Canederli, or bread dumplings, are a hearty and comforting dish that reflects the Alpine tradition of utilizing simple ingredients to create flavourful meals. Made from stale bread, milk, eggs and a medley of herbs, these dumplings are boiled to perfection and often served in a flavourful broth. Canederli are a delicious embodiment of the rustic and satisfying cuisine that warms the hearts of those in Vipiteno.

Alpine cheeses

Embark on a cheese lover's journey with Vipiteno's selection of Alpine cheeses. From tangy aged varieties to creamy fresh options, the town's cheese offerings represent the diversity of dairy craftsmanship in the region. Sample the distinct flavours of Puzzone di Moena, Grana Padano, or local Alpine varieties, paired perfectly with crusty bread or local honey.

Alpine herb infusions

Continue your culinary journey with Alpine herb infusions, a soothing and aromatic tradition in Vipiteno. Explore herbal teas crafted with locally sourced mountain herbs, such as juniper, mint and chamomile. These infusions not only offer a delightful end to a meal but also showcase the natural bounty of the Alpine meadows surrounding Vipiteno.

Vinschger Paarl

Break bread like a local with Vinschger Paarl, a traditional Alpine bread that embodies the rustic simplicity of Vipiteno's cuisine. This hearty bread, often made with a blend of whole grains and seeds, is a staple in local households. Enjoy it with local cheeses, cured meats, or simply toasted with a drizzle of olive oil for a genuine taste of Alpine life.

Krautkrapfen

Delight in the hearty goodness of Krautkrapfen, stuffed cabbage rolls filled with a savoury mixture of meat, rice and herbs. Slow-cooked to perfection, these rolls are often served with a dollop of tangy sauerkraut, creating a comforting and flavourful dish that resonates with the Alpine culinary heritage.

Immerse yourself in the culinary delights of Vipiteno, where each dish is a testament to the town's gastronomic legacy, embracing the flavours of the Alps and the warmth of Italian hospitality.

Mysteries of the Alps: Revealing Vipiteno's hidden delights

Beyond the well-trodden paths and renowned landmarks, Vipiteno harbours a collection of hidden gems that whisper tales of local secrets and captivating history. These lesser-known treasures add an extra layer of enchantment to the Alpine town, inviting intrepid explorers to uncover the nuances of Vipiteno's charm. Explore the hidden gems of Vipiteno, where each discovery unveils a unique facet of the town's cultural richness and Alpine allure.

Museo di Tesoro

Delve into the lesser-known Museo di tesoro, a treasure trove of religious artifacts and precious items housed within the Chiesa di San Giovanni. This hidden gem showcases a remarkable collection of ecclesiastical art, including intricately crafted gold and silver objects, ancient manuscripts and religious vestments. The museum provides a glimpse into the sacred heritage of Vipiteno, offering a quiet refuge for those seeking the town's hidden cultural treasures.

Pusterle di Vipiteno

Wander through the Pusterle di Vipiteno, a network of hidden alleyways that crisscross the town's medieval core. These charming passages, often overlooked by casual visitors, reveal glimpses of local life and architectural treasures. Lined with colourful facades, flower-filled balconies and unexpected views of the surrounding mountains, the Pusterle di Vipiteno hold the secrets of the town's intimate corners.

Fontana dei dodici

Discover the Fontana dei dodici, an elegant fountain hidden in the heart of Vipiteno's historical centre. Tucked away in a picturesque square, this hidden gem features a sculpted representation of the Twelve Apostles. The fountain, crafted in the Baroque style, offers a serene oasis amidst the town's vibrant streets, inviting contemplation and appreciation for its artistic beauty.

Via dei bottai

Stroll along the charming Via dei bottai, a hidden gem that winds through narrow cobblestone streets and medieval archways. Lined with artisan workshops and boutiques, this hidden alley captures the essence of Vipiteno's historic craftsmanship. Visitors can discover skilled coopers at work, creating traditional wooden barrels and casks. The timeless ambiance of Via dei Bottai invites exploration and reveals the town's artisanal soul.

Torre di Pozza

Ascend to the heights of Torre di Pozza, a hidden watchtower that stands as a testament to Vipiteno's medieval past. Although less frequented than other towers, Torre di Pozza offers panoramic views of the town and the surrounding mountains. The journey to this hidden gem involves a climb through narrow passages, adding a sense of adventure to the exploration of Vipiteno's skyline.

Casa Gries

Visit Casa Gries, a hidden architectural gem that exemplifies the elegant Jugendstil (Art Nouveau) style. Tucked away from the main thoroughfares, this historic house features decorative elements, stained glass windows and intricate detailing that reflect the artistic sensibilities of the early 20th century. Casa Gries stands as a testament to Vipiteno's architectural diversity and its ability to preserve hidden treasures.

Bunker Museum

Delve into the unexpected history of Vipiteno at the Bunker Museum, housed within a hidden World War II bunker. This unique museum offers a fascinating journey through the wartime experiences of the region, showcasing artifacts, photographs and interactive exhibits. The Bunker Museum provides a thought-provoking and hidden glimpse into Vipiteno's historical resilience.

Embark on a quest to uncover these hidden gems of Vipiteno, where each secret spot unveils a story, a piece of art, or a serene escape, adding layers of discovery to the tapestry of this enchanting Alpine town.

Summit Serenity: Embracing outdoor activities in Vipiteno

Vipiteno, surrounded by the majestic peaks of the Italian Alps, is a haven for outdoor enthusiasts seeking thrilling adventures amid breath-taking landscapes. From Alpine meadows to rugged mountain trails, the town offers a myriad of outdoor activities that cater to both the adrenaline seeker and the nature lover. Come along as we discover the diverse range of outdoor adventures in Vipiteno, where every ascent, descent and

scenic stroll promises an unforgettable experience in the embrace of the Alpine wilderness.

Hiking in the Sarentino Alps

Embark on a hiking odyssey through the Sarentino Alps, a pristine natural playground surrounding Vipiteno. Trails of varying difficulty levels weave through lush forests, Alpine meadows and panoramic ridges. One standout route is the Monte Cavallo trail, leading to breath-taking viewpoints overlooking Vipiteno and the surrounding valleys. Hiking in the Sarentino Alps is an immersive journey into the heart of the Alpine landscape.

Mountain biking along the Brenner cycle path

Saddle up for an exhilarating mountain biking adventure along the Brenner cycle path, a scenic route that connects Vipiteno with the Brenner Pass. The well-maintained trail offers a mix of challenging ascents and thrilling descents, with views of the Eisack River and the towering peaks of the Alps. Cyclists can explore charming villages, historical sites and enjoy the Alpine breeze as they traverse this picturesque route.

Rock climbing in Val di Vizze

For those seeking vertical thrills, Val di Vizze beckons with its impressive rock faces and challenging climbing routes. The sheer cliffs provide a playground for rock climbers of all skill levels. With professional guides available, adventurers can scale the granite walls while taking in panoramic vistas of the Vipiteno valley. Val di Vizze promises a rock-climbing experience that combines adrenaline with the awe-inspiring beauty of the Alpine surroundings.

Nordic walking through Alpine meadows

Immerse yourself in the tranquillity of Alpine meadows with Nordic walking, a popular activity in Vipiteno. The town offers a network of well-marked trails suitable for all fitness levels. Nordic walkers can enjoy the rhythmic exercise while surrounded by the scent of mountain flowers and the gentle sounds of nature. The practice combines fitness and serenity, providing an ideal way to explore the natural wonders surrounding Vipiteno.

Skiing and snowboarding in Racines-Giovo

Winter transforms Vipiteno into a snowy wonderland, inviting snow sports enthusiasts to Racines-Giovo for an unforgettable skiing and snowboarding experience. The ski resort boasts well-groomed slopes for all skill levels, from gentle descents for beginners to challenging runs for seasoned thrill-seekers. Surrounded by snow-covered peaks, Racines-Giovo offers a winter paradise where the joy of gliding down the slopes meets the breath-taking beauty of the Alpine landscape.

Paragliding from Mount Cavallo

Soar like an eagle with paragliding adventures launched from the heights of Mount Cavallo. Experienced pilots guide thrill-seekers on tandem flights, offering a unique perspective of Vipiteno and the surrounding mountains. As you glide through the crisp mountain air, the panoramic views unfold, providing an exhilarating experience that combines the freedom of flight with the stunning scenery of the Alps.

Eisack river rafting

Conquer the rapids of the Eisack River with thrilling white-water rafting adventures. The river, flowing through the picturesque valleys near Vipiteno, offers an exciting blend of adrenaline-pumping rapids and serene stretches. Guided rafting tours cater to both beginners and experienced rafters, providing a dynamic way to experience the natural beauty of the Alpine waterways.

Alpine horseback riding

Discover the beauty of Vipiteno on horseback with Alpine riding experiences. Trails wind through Alpine meadows, dense forests and offer breath-taking views of the surrounding peaks. Whether you're a seasoned rider or a novice, guided horseback excursions provide a unique perspective of the landscape, allowing riders to connect with nature while exploring the diverse terrain surrounding Vipiteno.

Via ferrata on the Hoher Lorenzen

Conquer the vertical challenges of the Hoher Lorenzen via ferrata, an exhilarating climbing route with breath-taking exposure. The via ferrata offers a combination of iron ladders, suspended bridges and challenging rock faces, providing a thrilling ascent to panoramic viewpoints. This adventure on the Hoher Lorenzen rewards climbers with a sense of accomplishment and awe-inspiring vistas of the surrounding Alpine peaks.

Golfing at golf club Sterzing

Tee off amidst the Alpine scenery at the Golf Club Sterzing, a hidden gem for golf enthusiasts. Nestled in the valley, the golf course offers stunning views of the surrounding mountains as players navigate its fairways and greens. The challenging course is complemented by the crisp mountain air, creating an idyllic setting for a round of golf in the heart of the Alps.

Vipiteno's outdoor activities cater to a diverse range of interests, making it a year-round destination for those eager to explore the splendours of the Alpine wilderness. Whether ascending mountain peaks or gliding down snowy slopes, the outdoor adventures in Vipiteno promise unforgettable moments amidst nature's grandeur.

Festive Peaks: Embracing Vipiteno's Alpine Traditions

Vipiteno, nestled in the heart of the Italian Alps, is not only a haven for natural beauty but also a town deeply rooted in rich cultural traditions and festive celebrations. Throughout the year, Vipiteno comes alive with a tapestry of local customs, time-honoured rituals and vibrant festivals that reflect the town's heritage. Let us explore the captivating traditions and festivals of Vipiteno, where each event offers a glimpse into the community's spirit and the Alpine traditions that have endured through generations.

Sterzinger fischfeier (July)

The Sterzinger Fischfeier, or Sterzing Fish Festival, is an annual event that pays homage to the town's historical fishing traditions. The festival transforms the streets into a culinary haven, featuring stalls offering a variety of freshwater fish dishes. Locals and visitors gather to savour the flavours of Alpine trout and other delectable fish preparations, accompanied by traditional music and lively festivities.

Schafabtrieb (September)

Witness a pastoral spectacle during the Schafabtrieb, or sheep descent, an autumnal tradition that celebrates the return of sheep from the high mountain pastures. Shepherds guide their flocks through the town's streets, adorned with traditional Alpine bells and colourful decorations. The Schafabtrieb is a charming display of Vipiteno's connection to its agricultural roots and the harmonious coexistence of town and countryside.

Altjahrswoche (December)

Altjahrswoche, or old year's week, is a unique tradition in Vipiteno that spans the days between Christmas and New Year's Eve. During this time, locals engage in various customs, including the burning of the 'Altjahrsfeuer' (Old year's fire) to symbolize the end of the year. The week is marked by communal gatherings, festive meals and a sense of reflection as the town bids farewell to the old year and welcomes the new one.

Krampuslauf (December)

Embrace the darker side of Alpine folklore with the Krampuslauf, a centuries-old tradition that takes place in early December. Men adorned in elaborate Krampus costumes roam the streets, embodying mythical creatures that accompany St. Nicholas. The Krampuslauf is a thrilling spectacle where locals and visitors gather to witness the lively parade, complete with menacing masks, jingling bells and a festive atmosphere that adds a touch of the mysterious to the holiday season.

Bauerngartl (August)

Experience the lively spirit of Vipiteno's rural traditions during the Bauerngartl, or Farmers' Parade. This colourful procession showcases the agricultural heritage of the region. Farmers, adorned in traditional attire, lead a parade of decorated floats, livestock and marching bands through the town's streets. The Bauerngartl is a vibrant celebration that highlights the importance of agriculture in Vipiteno's cultural identity.

Sunnseitnfest (August)

Embrace the warmth of summer during the Sunnseitnfest, or Sunny side festival. This lively event celebrates the sun-drenched days of the Alpine summer with music, dance and outdoor activities. Locals and visitors come together to enjoy open-air concerts, street performances and a joyful atmosphere that encapsulates the sunnier side of Vipiteno's seasonal charm.

Festum Tiburtii (August)

Vipiteno commemorates its patron saint, St. Tiburtius, with the Festum Tiburtii, a religious festival in which the town comes together for a solemn procession, featuring the statue of St. Tiburtius carried through the streets by locals in traditional attire. The festival combines religious rituals with a sense of community, providing a glimpse into the town's deep-rooted spiritual heritage.

Weihnachtsmarkt (December)

Immerse yourself in the enchanting ambiance of the Weihnachtsmarkt, Vipiteno's traditional Christmas Market. The market features festive stalls adorned with twinkling lights, offering handcrafted gifts, local treats and seasonal delights against the backdrop of snow-covered mountains. The aroma of mulled wine and the sounds of Christmas carols create a magical atmosphere, making the Weihnachtsmarkt a cherished annual tradition.

These local traditions and festivals weave a vibrant tapestry of culture and celebration in Vipiteno, inviting visitors to immerse themselves in the town's rich heritage and Alpine charm throughout the changing seasons.

Insider's Alp: Expert advice for exploring Vipiteno's charms

Nestled in the embrace of the Italian Alps, Vipiteno beckons travellers with its timeless charm and Alpine allure. Whether you're an adventure seeker, a cultural enthusiast, or a nature lover, this enchanting town has something for everyone. To ensure a seamless and memorable journey, we present a collection of travel tips that will guide you through the cobblestone streets, picturesque landscapes and rich cultural experiences of Vipiteno. From outdoor adventures to local customs, these tips will enhance your visit to this Alpine gem.

Embrace Alpine time

Vipiteno operates on its own rhythm, often referred to as 'Alpine time'. Embrace the leisurely pace of life, allowing yourself to savour each moment. Whether enjoying a coffee in a charming café or taking a stroll through the historic streets, give in to the unhurried tempo and relish the beauty of the present.

Pack layers for Alpine weather

The Alpine weather can be unpredictable, with temperature variations throughout the day. Pack layers to accommodate chilly mornings, warm afternoons and cool evenings. A waterproof jacket and sturdy walking shoes are essential for exploring the diverse landscapes, from the town's cobblestone streets to the mountain trails.

Explore on foot

Vipiteno's compact size makes it an ideal destination for exploring on foot. Wander through the medieval streets, discover hidden alleys and soak in the panoramic views of the surrounding mountains. Comfortable walking shoes are your best companions for immersing yourself in the town's enchanting atmosphere.

Engage with locals

Connect with the warm-hearted locals to enhance your Vipiteno experience. Engage in friendly conversations at local shops, restaurants and markets. The people of Vipiteno are proud of their town and are often delighted to share insights, recommendations and stories that add a personal touch to your journey.

Visit off-peak for quiet moments

For a more intimate experience, consider visiting Vipiteno during the off-peak seasons. Spring and fall offer quieter streets, allowing you to enjoy the town's beauty with fewer crowds. This is an excellent time for nature enthusiasts and those seeking a peaceful escape.

Learn basic Italian and German phrases

While many locals speak both Italian and German, learning a few basic phrases in each language can enhance your interactions. The effort to communicate in the local languages is often appreciated and adds a personal touch to your cultural exchange.

Respect Alpine wildlife

If you're exploring the surrounding mountains, be mindful of Alpine wildlife. Keep a respectful distance from animals, follow designated trails and adhere to any environmental guidelines. Responsible exploration ensures the preservation of Vipiteno's natural beauty for generations to come.

Experience Christmas magic

If you find yourself in Vipiteno during the winter season, don't miss the magical atmosphere of the Weihnachtsmarkt (Christmas Market). The snow-covered setting, twinkling lights and festive ambiance create a winter wonderland that captures the spirit of the holidays.

Stay in a traditional guesthouse

Enhance your cultural immersion by choosing a traditional guesthouse for your accommodation. These cosy establishments often reflect the charm of Vipiteno's architecture and offer a more authentic experience, complete with warm hospitality and local insights.

As you embark on your journey to Vipiteno, let these travel tips be your companions, guiding you through the nuances of this Alpine town. Whether you're seeking adventure, cultural exploration, or moments of tranquillity, Vipiteno awaits with open arms and a wealth of experiences to discover.

Vipiteno's farewell: Concluding the Alpine adventure with reflections

Leaving Vipiteno behind does not mark the end of your Alpine adventure but rather the continuation of a journey shaped by the cultural nuances and breath-taking landscapes of this Alpine jewel. The tales of medieval splendour, the warmth of the locals and the panoramic vistas from the surrounding mountains become treasured souvenirs.

As you traverse beyond the Alpine horizon, the closing thoughts on Vipiteno are a prelude to the next chapter in your exploration of South Tyrol. May the Alpine spirit, the architectural elegance and the alchemy of Austrian-Italian influences discovered in Vipiteno become threads woven into the fabric of your Alpine tapestry. As you step away from the cobbled streets, may the alpine echoes accompany you, a reminder of Vipiteno's enduring allure amidst the grandeur of the Dolomites.

Tellaro: Tales from tranquil shores

Whispers of Tellaro: A prelude to enchanted seascapes

Nestled along the rugged cliffs of the Ligurian coast, Tellaro emerges as a coastal gem, a place where time seems to slow down and the whispers of the sea blend seamlessly with the melody of everyday life and located just 10 kilometres south of Lerici. Situated at an altitude of approximately 70 meters above sea level, Tellaro provides a tranquil retreat for visitors seeking relaxation and natural beauty amidst its coastal splendour.

This picturesque fishing village, with its pastel-hued houses perched on the cliffs, invites travellers to step into a world where maritime charm meets timeless elegance. As you navigate the narrow alleyways adorned with vibrant bougainvillea and overlook the azure expanse of the Ligurian Sea, Tellaro unfolds as a storybook destination, where every corner reveals a new chapter in the coastal saga. This introduction beckons you to embark on a journey through the enchanting landscapes of Tellaro, where the sea breeze carries tales of seafaring traditions and the sun-drenched cliffs hold the secrets of a coastal haven steeped in history and maritime allure.

Echoes of antiquity: Tellaro's time-weathered tale

Immersed in the rich tapestry of Italian history, Tellaro bears witness to centuries of maritime heritage and cultural evolution. Tracing its origins to ancient times, this coastal haven served as a strategic outpost for maritime trade and defence. The town's historical significance is palpable in its architecture, where weathered stone facades and medieval structures speak of a bygone era. Tellaro's maritime legacy is interwoven with tales of seafaring exploits, pirate invasions and the resilience of a community tethered to the sea.

One of the notable historical landmarks is the Church of San Giorgio, an architectural gem dating back to the 13th century. Its ancient stones echo with the stories of sailors seeking divine protection before venturing into the unpredictable waters. The town's medieval layout, with narrow alleyways and defensive walls, reflects its strategic importance in safeguarding the Ligurian coast.

Tellaro's historical significance extends to its role in the cultural and artistic movements that shaped the region. Artists, poets and writers have found inspiration in its timeless charm, leaving an indelible mark on the town's cultural narrative. Today, wandering through Tellaro is like stepping into a living museum, where each cobblestone tells a story and the sea breeze carries the whispers of a maritime history that continues to enchant visitors from around the world.

Coastal elegance: Unravelling Tellaro's cultural symphony

Tellaro, with its timeless charm and intimate coastal setting, is a cradle of Ligurian culture that beckons visitors into the heart of Italian maritime traditions. The pulse of local life in this enchanting village beats to the rhythm of the sea, reflected in the bustling harbour where fishermen mend their nets and share tales of the day's catch. The streets, adorned with vibrant bougainvillea and adorned facades, set the stage for a captivating cultural experience.

The gastronomic scene of Tellaro is a celebration of maritime flavours, where local trattorias serve up the day's freshest catches amidst an ambiance of conviviality. Traditional festivals, deeply rooted in local customs, punctuate the calendar, offering a glimpse into the community's rituals and celebrations. As the evening sun casts a golden glow over the Ligurian coast, the sound of laughter and music emanates from tucked-away piazzas, inviting visitors to partake in the warmth of Tellaro's local culture-a harmonious blend of seafaring heritage, culinary delights and the enduring spirit of coastal camaraderie.

Seaside Charms: Unveiling Tellaro's Enchanted Landmarks

Nestled along the rugged coastline of the Italian Riviera, Tellaro enchants visitors with its timeless beauty, quaint charm and rich maritime heritage. From ancient churches to scenic viewpoints, every corner of this picturesque fishing village tells a story waiting to be explored. Join me as we embark on a journey through Tellaro's most iconic landmarks and points of interest, uncovering the hidden gems and cultural treasures that make this coastal gem a must-visit destination on the Ligurian coast.

Punta Bianca

Punta Bianca, the iconic white-tipped rock that juts into the sea, is a natural landmark that defines Tellaro's coastal silhouette. This distinctive geological formation, kissed by the sun and caressed by the waves, serves as a poetic backdrop to the town's seaside vistas. It stands as a silent guardian, bearing witness to the ebb and flow of time along the Ligurian shore.

The Castle and Defensive Walls

The remnants of Tellaro's medieval defensive walls and castle are living echoes of a time when the town stood as a sentinel against maritime threats. As you stroll along these weathered fortifications, you'll be transported to an era of watchtowers, protective ramparts and a community united in safeguarding its coastal haven.

Piazza del commune

The beating heart of Tellaro, Piazza del commune is a charming square surrounded by pastel-coloured buildings, local cafes and artisan shops. This lively hub is where locals and visitors converge, savouring the vibrant atmosphere, sipping espresso and immersing themselves in the authentic pulse of Tellaro's daily life.

Church of San Giorgio

Perched atop a cliff overlooking the Ligurian Sea, the Church of San Giorgio stands as a testament to Tellaro's medieval past. Dating back to the 13th century, its ancient stones echo with the prayers of seafarers seeking protection before embarking on perilous journeys. The church's commanding presence and panoramic views make it a landmark that encapsulates the town's spiritual and maritime essence.

The maritime museum

The maritime museum of Tellaro is a treasure trove of nautical artifacts, maps and tales of seafaring exploits. Housed in a quaint building near the harbour, the museum offers a captivating journey through the maritime history of the region. It's a must-visit for those eager to delve into the town's deep connection with the sea.

Via Colombo

Via Colombo, the main street winding through Tellaro, is a picturesque thoroughfare that captures the essence of Ligurian charm. Lined with boutiques, gelaterias and local shops, it invites you to meander through its timeless ambiance, where each step reveals hidden corners and delightful surprises.

The seafront promenade

The seafront promenade of Tellaro is a scenic pathway that hugs the coastline, offering breath-taking views of the Ligurian Sea and Punta Bianca. Lined with benches and shaded by ancient trees, it's a tranquil space where you can savour the sea breeze, watch fishing boats bob in the harbour and lose yourself in the serenity of coastal living.

As you explore these landmarks and points of interest, you'll find that each holds a key to unlocking a different facet of Tellaro's story-a story written in the language of the sea, etched into its architecture and woven into the fabric of everyday life.

Epicurean waves: Savouring Tellaro's coastal culinary symphony

Tellaro, a seaside haven perched on the rugged cliffs of the Italian Riviera, offers not only mesmerizing coastal vistas but also a delectable array of culinary delights. The village's maritime heritage is tastefully reflected in its cuisine, where fresh catches from the Ligurian Sea take centre stage. From seafood delights that capture the essence of the Mediterranean to locally inspired dishes that pay homage to Ligurian flavours, Tellaro invites you on a gastronomic journey that harmonizes with the soothing sounds of the waves. Join us as we explore the culinary treasures that make dining in Tellaro a celebration of coastal authenticity.

Acciughe al Verde

Delight your taste buds with Acciughe al Verde, a traditional Ligurian dish featuring anchovies immersed in a vibrant green sauce made with parsley, garlic and olive oil. The combination of the briny anchovies and the herbaceous sauce offers a burst of coastal flavours that is both bold and refreshing.

Frittura di paranza

Indulge in the Frittura di paranza, a seafood lover's dream come true. This dish showcases a variety of small, freshly caught fish, such as anchovies, squid and shrimp, lightly battered and fried to crispy perfection. The Frittura di Paranza is often served with a wedge of lemon, adding a zesty touch to this delightful seaside delicacy.

Pansoti al sugo di noci

Pansoti al sugo di noci is a regional pasta dish that features triangular-shaped ravioli filled with a flavourful mixture of herbs, cheese and greens. What makes this dish truly special is the walnut sauce that accompanies it, adding a creamy and nutty dimension to the pasta, creating a symphony of textures and tastes.

Cima alla Ligure

Experience the heritage of Ligurian cuisine with Cima alla Ligure, a dish that showcases the culinary artistry of the region. It consists of a deboned and stuffed veal breast, cooked to perfection and served cold. The filling typically includes a mix of meats, eggs, cheese and herbs, creating a savoury and satisfying centrepiece.

Trofie al pesto Genovese

Savour the quintessential Ligurian pasta, Trofie al pesto Genovese, where hand-rolled pasta is paired with a vibrant basil-based pesto sauce. The simplicity of this dish allows the flavours of fresh basil, garlic, pine nuts and Parmesan to shine, creating a palate-pleasing symphony that captures the essence of Ligurian gastronomy.

Cappon magro

Cappon magro is a Ligurian seafood salad that epitomizes the bounty of the Mediterranean. This layered dish features a variety of seafood, including lobster, shrimp and anchovies, arranged on a bed of vegetables and hardtack soaked in a rich sauce. The result is a visually stunning and sumptuous dish that reflects the coastal abundance of Tellaro.

Stoccafisso accomodato

Embrace the flavours of Tellaro with Stoccafisso accomodato, a dish cantered around dried and salted codfish. The cod is rehydrated and cooked with potatoes, tomatoes, olives and capers, creating a savoury and hearty maritime dish that pays homage to the village's seafaring traditions.

Focaccia Ligure

No exploration of Ligurian cuisine is complete without savouring Focaccia Ligure. In Tellaro, this beloved flatbread is adorned with a generous drizzle of extra-virgin olive oil and sprinkled with coarse sea salt. The result is a golden and crispy delicacy that serves as the perfect accompaniment to a seaside meal.

Limoncino Ligure

Toast to the coastal flavours of Tellaro with Limoncino Ligure, a lemon-infused liqueur that captures the essence of the region. Sip on this refreshing digestif, made from locally sourced lemons, as you bask in the sea breeze and the lingering flavours of your Tellaro culinary adventure.

Torta di Riso

Conclude your culinary journey in Tellaro with Torta di Riso, a traditional Ligurian rice cake. This delightful dessert combines rice, sugar, eggs and lemon zest, resulting in a light and fragrant treat. Often enjoyed with a dusting of powdered sugar, Torta di Riso captures the sweet essence of Ligurian cuisine.

In Tellaro, each culinary delight is a tribute to the village's maritime heritage, a symphony of flavours that resonates with the rhythm of the Ligurian Sea. From pasta dishes that showcase the simplicity of local ingredients to seafood delights that mirror the abundance of the Mediterranean, dining in Tellaro is a sensory celebration that immerses you in the coastal charm of this Ligurian gem.

Whispers of secrecy: Unveiling Tellaro's maritime treasures

Beyond the well-trodden paths and famous landmarks, Tellaro unveils a world of hidden gems-quiet corners, secluded spots and secret havens that whisper tales of authenticity and charm. These hidden treasures, known to locals and intrepid explorers, beckon you to venture off the beaten track and discover the nuances of Tellaro's soul. From hidden coves kissed by the Ligurian Sea to tucked-away squares adorned with bougainvillea, each gem encapsulates the town's enchanting essence, inviting you to uncover the secrets that make Tellaro an undiscovered paradise.

Piazzetta del Mar

Tucked away from the bustling thoroughfares, Piazzetta del Mar is a hidden square that offers a breath-taking panorama of the Ligurian Sea. With a backdrop of pastel-hued buildings and the rhythmic sounds of lapping waves, this secret oasis invites you to indulge in moments of serenity and awe-inspiring beauty.

Grotta di Byron

Whispering tales of poetic inspiration, Grotta di Byron is a hidden sea cave accessible by boat, revealing a magical world of crystalline waters and natural wonders. It is said that Lord Byron sought refuge in this cave for contemplation, making it a haven for those seeking a quiet escape amidst nature's embrace.

Spiaggia di Fiascherino

Discover Spiaggia di Fiascherino, a hidden beach nestled between rugged cliffs and bathed in the golden glow of the Mediterranean sun. Accessible by a scenic walk along the coastline, this secluded gem offers a peaceful retreat, where the sound of gently lapping waves and the soft touch of warm sand create a haven of tranquillity.

Belvedere di Montemarcello

For panoramic vistas and hidden viewpoints, venture to Belvedere di Montemarcello. Accessed by a scenic trail, this hidden gem provides sweeping views of Tellaro, the Gulf of La Spezia and the rugged Ligurian coastline. It's a secret spot that rewards the intrepid explorer with unparalleled beauty.

Tramonti di Tellaro

Experience the magic of sunset at Tramonti di Tellaro, a hidden spot where the sky transforms into a canvas of warm hues. Away from the crowds, this vantage point offers a quiet retreat to witness the sun's descent behind the horizon, casting a golden glow over the town and the shimmering sea.

Vicolo degli Innamorati

Romance comes to life in Vicolo degli Innamorati, a hidden alleyway adorned with love-themed murals and quaint details. As you wander through this atmospheric passageway, you'll find yourself immersed in the romantic ambiance that permeates Tellaro, capturing the essence of love and connection.

Tellaro's Hidden Gems beckon you to embrace the spirit of discovery, inviting you to peel back the layers of the town's charm and unearth the secrets that make it an authentic and timeless destination. As you weave through hidden alleyways and stumble upon these whispered treasures, you'll find that Tellaro's allure lies not just in what meets the eye but in the intimate stories waiting to be uncovered.

Riviera reverie: Outdoor pursuits in Tellaro's coastal playground

Bathed in the golden glow of the Italian Riviera, Tellaro extends an invitation to explore its outdoor wonders-a realm where the azure sea meets rugged cliffs and nature unfolds in a symphony of breath-taking landscapes. Beyond its medieval charm and hidden alleys, Tellaro unveils a playground for outdoor enthusiasts. From invigorating coastal hikes to tranquil moments by the sea, each outdoor activity promises to immerse you in the untamed beauty of the Ligurian coast. Embark on a journey where the allure of Tellaro's outdoors transcends the ordinary, inviting you to savour the magic of the Mediterranean in every step and breath.

Coastal hiking trails

Discover the dramatic beauty of Tellaro's coastline through scenic hiking trails. Coastal paths wind along cliffs adorned with Mediterranean flora, offering panoramic views of the Ligurian Sea. A favourite route leads to the neighbouring village of Montemarcello, rewarding hikers with vistas of the Gulf of La Spezia and the Apuan Alps.

Kayaking in the Ligurian Sea

Embark on a maritime adventure with kayaking excursions along the Ligurian Sea. Glide through crystal-clear waters, exploring hidden coves and sea caves. Kayaking allows you to intimately connect with Tellaro's coastal charm, offering a unique perspective of the town's cliffs and secluded beaches.

Snorkelling and scuba diving

Beneath the surface of the Ligurian Sea lies a world of underwater wonders awaiting exploration. Engage in snorkelling or scuba diving adventures to discover vibrant marine life, underwater rock formations and the captivating biodiversity of the protected marine area surrounding Tellaro.

Bike rides through olive groves

Explore the enchanting countryside surrounding Tellaro with leisurely bike rides. Follow paths through ancient olive groves, charming hamlets and vineyard-draped hills. Biking allows you to absorb the peaceful ambiance of the Ligurian landscape while discovering the hidden treasures of the hinterland.

Sailing along the Gulf of Poets

Set sail from Tellaro's harbour and experience the Gulf of Poets from the perspective of the sea. Sailing excursions offer a leisurely escape, allowing you to bask in the coastal breeze, admire the rugged shoreline and revel in the timeless allure of the Ligurian coast.

Rock climbing in Monte Marcello

For the adventurous spirit, Monte Marcello provides a natural playground for rock climbing enthusiasts. The limestone cliffs offer a variety of routes suitable for different skill levels, providing a thrilling and panoramic ascent with views of the Ligurian Sea as a reward.

Yoga by the sea

Savour moments of tranquillity with yoga sessions set against the backdrop of the Ligurian coast. Tellaro's outdoor spaces, from seafront promenades to hidden squares, become serene sanctuaries where you can engage in rejuvenating yoga practices, harmonizing mind, body and spirit.

Sunset picnics on Punta Bianca

Indulge in the romance of Tellaro's sunsets with picnics on Punta Bianca. This hidden gem offers a peaceful setting for an evening reprieve, where you can unwind, savour local delicacies and watch the sun dip below the horizon, casting a warm glow over the Ligurian landscape.

Tellaro's outdoor activities are an invitation to weave the story of your visit into the fabric of the Ligurian landscape. Whether you seek adrenaline-pumping adventures or serene moments of contemplation, the town's natural wonders promise an immersive experience that resonates with the soul of the Mediterranean.

Seaside spectacle: Tellaro's festive tapestry of local traditions

Tellaro, with its timeless charm and maritime soul, comes alive throughout the year with a tapestry of local traditions and festivals that reflect the town's rich cultural heritage. These celebrations, deeply rooted in Ligurian traditions, invite visitors to witness the vibrancy of local life, where the rhythms of the sea and the heartbeat of community spirit harmonize. From ancient religious processions to lively carnivals, each tradition and festival paints a vivid portrait of Tellaro's collective identity-a captivating blend of seafaring traditions, culinary delights and joyous camaraderie that defines this coastal haven.

Festa di San Giuseppe (March)

Tellaro pays homage to Saint Joseph with Festa di San Giuseppe. The festivities include religious processions, where the statue of Saint Joseph is paraded through the town's streets, accompanied by traditional hymns and the aroma of lilies-the saint's symbolic flower. The festival reflects the town's deep connection to its patron saint and the onset of spring.

Sagra del Totano (August)

Sagra del Totano is a festival dedicated to the local delicacy of squid. The town's squares transform into culinary stages where chefs showcase creative squid dishes, from grilled calamari to savoury squid ink pasta. The festival not only celebrates maritime gastronomy but also honours the skill of local fishermen.

Festa di San Lorenzo (August)

Amidst the summer's warmth, Tellaro celebrates Festa di San Lorenzo in honour of Saint Lawrence. The festival features a lively procession, traditional music and a vibrant atmosphere as locals come together to pay tribute to their patron saint. The flickering lights of bonfires and the night sky illuminate the festive spirit.

Processione del Mare (August)

Processione del Mare is a unique maritime procession that honours the sea in which locals carry a statue of the Madonna from the Church of San Giorgio to the waterfront, where fishing boats decked in festive lights join the procession. It's a captivating spectacle that encapsulates Tellaro's reverence for the sea.

Palio Marinaro (August)

Tellaro's maritime prowess takes centre stage with the Palio Marinaro. This historical regatta pits the town's neighbourhoods against each other in a thrilling boat race, echoing centuries-old traditions. The colourful spectacle unfolds in the azure waters of the Ligurian Sea, showcasing seafaring skill and community pride.

Sagra della Focaccia (September)

Sagra della Focaccia is a celebration of the region's beloved flatbread. The town's ovens produce an array of focaccia variations, from traditional olive-topped delights to creative interpretations. The festival is a culinary journey that brings locals and visitors together to savour the flavours of Ligurian baking.

Processione di Santa Lucia (December)

Tellaro reveres Santa Lucia with a solemn procession that winds through the town's decorated streets. The statue of Santa Lucia is carried with reverence, accompanied by candlelight and hymns, creating a serene atmosphere that marks the beginning of the Christmas season in Tellaro.

Notte delle Stelle (December)

As the year draws to a close, Tellaro sparkles with the Notte delle Stelle, a festive event that transforms the town into a twinkling wonderland. The narrow streets and squares come alive with Christmas lights, decorations and joyful gatherings. Notte delle Stelle is a magical prelude to the holiday season, casting a warm glow over Tellaro's cobbled alleys.

Tellaro's Local Traditions and Festivals weave a cultural tapestry that invites you to immerse yourself in the rhythms of community life. Whether joining in a vibrant carnival parade, savouring seafood delights, or witnessing the maritime processions, each celebration provides a glimpse into the heart of Tellaro's collective spirit-a spirit shaped by the sea and illuminated by the traditions that have endured through generations

Seafarer's secrets: Navigating Tellaro's coastal charm with finesse

Embarking on a journey to Tellaro is an entrancing venture into the heart of Ligurian coastal allure. To ensure your visit is a seamless and enriching experience, these travel tips serve as your compass, guiding you through the enchanting lanes, hidden gems and maritime traditions that define this coastal haven. From practical insights on transportation to the best vantage points for panoramic views, these tips are crafted to enhance your exploration of Tellaro-a destination where time slows and the whispers of the sea beckon you into a realm of timeless beauty.

Getting there

Tellaro is accessible by car, with parking available on the outskirts of the town. Alternatively, you can arrive by boat or bus from nearby towns such as Lerici. While Tellaro's narrow streets make driving challenging, the pedestrian-friendly layout encourages exploration on foot.

Navigating the streets

Wander through Tellaro's charming streets with comfortable walking shoes. The town's intricate layout, characterized by narrow alleys and staircases, is best explored on foot. Be prepared for cobblestone paths and allow yourself to get lost in the labyrinth of hidden corners.

Best time to visit

The ideal time to visit Tellaro is during the spring and summer months when the weather is mild and outdoor activities are in full swing. However, the quieter months of autumn offer a more tranquil experience, revealing a different side of Tellaro's coastal charm.

Lodging choices

Accommodations in Tellaro range from boutique hotels to charming bed and breakfasts. Consider staying in a waterfront property to wake up to the sound of the sea. Booking in advance is recommended, especially during peak tourist seasons.

Dining by the sea

Savour local culinary delights in Tellaro's waterfront trattorias. Fresh seafood, homemade pasta and Ligurian specialties await. Don't miss the chance to dine al fresco, immersing yourself in the coastal ambiance.

Seafaring excursions

Explore the Ligurian Sea with boat excursions departing from Tellaro's harbour. Whether it's a sailing adventure, kayaking along the coast, or a fishing expedition, these maritime experiences provide a unique perspective of Tellaro's beauty.

Respect local traditions

Respect the town's traditions and festivals, as they play a significant role in Tellaro's cultural identity. If your visit coincides with a local celebration, immerse yourself in the festivities and witness the vibrant spirit of community life.

Pack essentials
Pack essentials such as sunscreen, a hat and comfortable clothing for coastal exploration. A camera is a must to capture the scenic beauty of Tellaro and a reusable water bottle will keep you hydrated as you traverse the town's captivating landscapes.

Local etiquette

Engage with locals respectfully, as Tellaro maintains a close-knit community atmosphere. Learn a few basic Italian phrases and embrace the relaxed pace of life that characterizes this coastal gem.

As you navigate Tellaro's coastal charm with finesse, these travel tips will enhance your experience, allowing you to embrace the town's maritime poetry and create lasting memories along the Ligurian shore. Whether you're captivated by ancient traditions, enchanted by hidden corners, or simply savouring the sea breeze, Tellaro beckons you into a world where every moment is a celebration of coastal living.

Tales of the tide: Concluding the Tellaro odyssey with coastal whispers

As you bid adieu to Tellaro, the essence of its coastal legacy becomes a cherished keepsake, resonating in the sound of distant waves and the play of sunlight on the sea. The village's time-weathered charm, maritime traditions and the warmth of its community become tales carried forward in your own narrative.

Tellaro's coastal beauty, with its hidden coves and sunsets casting a golden glow over the horizon, leaves an indelible mark on your journey. As you venture beyond the Ligurian Riviera, the closing thoughts on Tellaro are not just an end but a continuation-a continuation of the seaside symphony, the whispered tales and the enduring magic of a coastal haven that remains alive in the heart.

Cinque Terre: Cliffside symphony by the sea

Jay Chandarana

Maritime musings: A prelude to Cinque Terre's seaside splendour

Nestled along the rugged coastline of the Italian Riviera, Cinque Terre stands as a captivating testament to the harmonious interplay between nature and human endeavour. Literally translating to 'Five Lands', this UNESCO World Heritage site comprises five enchanting villages: Monterosso al Mare, Vernazza, Corniglia and Manarola and Riomaggiore. Each village is a jewel in its own right, characterized by colourful buildings clinging to steep cliffs, overlooking the azure waters of the Ligurian Sea. Located within close proximity to major cities such as Genoa and Florence, the Cinque Terre is accessible by train, boat, or car. The collective charm of Cinque Terre lies in its unique topography, where terraced vineyards, olive groves and citrus orchards cascade down the hillsides, creating a vibrant mosaic of colours and textures. With altitudes ranging from sea level to approximately 200 meters, the Cinque Terre provides ample opportunities for hiking, photography and cultural exploration in one of Italy's most stunning coastal regions.

Cinque Terre has become a magnet for travellers seeking an authentic Italian experience. Visitors can meander through narrow cobblestone streets, savouring local delicacies and exploring centuries-old churches and watchtowers. The breath-taking hiking trails that connect the villages offer unparalleled panoramic views, allowing adventurers to immerse themselves in the timeless beauty of this coastal haven. Cinque Terre, with its captivating blend of natural splendour and cultural richness, stands as a testament to the enduring allure of the Italian coastline.

Join me on a journey through this enchanting coastal paradise, where every twist and turn reveals a new adventure.

Riviera reminiscence: Cinque Terre's time-honoured legacy

Cinque Terre's historical significance unfolds like a rich tapestry woven with the threads of maritime trade, strategic importance and resilient coastal communities. The origins of the five villages can be traced back to medieval times, with the first settlements emerging as a response to the need for protection from pirate raids and other external threats. The coastal location of Cinque Terre proved strategic for maritime trade and the villages flourished as vital hubs for shipping and fishing during the Middle Ages.

Over the centuries, the resilient inhabitants carved terraced landscapes into the steep cliffs, creating an intricate system of agricultural cultivation that sustained their communities. Today, Cinque Terre's historical significance is not only a testament to the resilience of its people but also an open book inviting travellers to explore the layers of history embedded in its picturesque streets and scenic landscapes.

Mediterranean marvels: Discovering the beauty of Cinque Terre

Cinque Terre's local culture is a captivating blend of tradition, community spirit and a deep-rooted connection to the stunning natural surroundings. The residents, known as Cinque Terresi, take immense pride in preserving their cultural heritage, which has evolved over centuries of isolation and resilience. One of the most prominent aspects of local culture is the emphasis on community and collective identity. The five villages, although distinct, share common values and a strong sense of solidarity, fostered by their historically isolated geography. This communal spirit is evident in various aspects of daily life, from traditional festivals to communal agricultural practices that have been passed down through generations.

The gastronomic delights of Cinque Terre are an integral part of its local culture. Fresh seafood, locally grown olives and grapes from the terraced vineyards contribute to a culinary experience that reflects the region's maritime and agrarian heritage. Visitors can indulge in the flavours of Ligurian cuisine, characterized by dishes such as pesto, anchovies and the renowned Sciacchetrà wine. Artisanal crafts also play a role in preserving the local identity, with handmade goods showcasing the skills and creativity of the residents. From intricately crafted lace to vibrant ceramics, these crafts serve as both cultural artifacts and sources of livelihood for local artisans. Cinque Terre's local culture is an immersive journey into a way of life shaped by a deep connection to the land and a resilient spirit that continues to thrive in the face of modernization.

Echoes of elegance: Unravelling the enchantment of Cinque Terre

Cinque Terre, a string of five picturesque villages perched along the rugged Italian Riviera, is a treasure trove of coastal beauty and cultural richness. Each village, with its distinct character and colourful facades, boasts a collection of landmarks that tell the tales of centuries past. As you embark on your journey through the enchanting Cinque Terre, here is a guide to the most notable landmarks and points of interest that grace these cliffside communities, offering a glimpse into their history, traditions and breath-taking landscapes.

Vernazza's Piazza Marconi

Piazza Marconi in Vernazza is a lively square that serves as the heart of the village. Lined with colourful buildings, cafes and shops, the piazza is a bustling gathering place for locals and visitors alike. It offers a vibrant atmosphere and a perfect vantage point for admiring the coastal scenery.

Corniglia's Terrace of Santa Maria

The Terrace of Santa Maria in Corniglia is a panoramic viewpoint that provides stunning vistas of the sea and the surrounding vineyards. Accessible by a scenic walk, the terrace is an ideal spot to savour the tranquillity of Cinque Terre's landscapes.

Manarola's Via dell'Amore

Via dell'Amore, or Lover's lane, is a scenic coastal path that connects the villages of Manarola and Riomaggiore. Known for its breath-taking views of the Ligurian Sea, the path is adorned with colourful love locks and provides a romantic setting for a leisurely stroll while enjoying the captivating vistas.

Corniglia's Tower of Corniglia

The Tower of Corniglia, located on the highest point of the village, is a historic structure that once served as a lookout tower for defence against pirate attacks. Today, it stands as a symbol of Corniglia's maritime past and offers panoramic views of the surroundings.

Riomaggiore's Marina

Riomaggiore's picturesque marina is a captivating landmark where colourful boats bob in the turquoise waters. This coastal haven invites visitors to relax by the waterfront, enjoy the vibrant ambiance and soak in the charm of Cinque Terre's coastal lifestyle.

Monterosso's Giant Statue and Convent of Monterosso al Mare

Standing tall along the coastline of Monterosso is Il Gigante, a colossal statue of Neptune, the Roman god of the sea. Nearby, the Convent of Monterosso al Mare is a historic site that dates back to the 17th century, offering a serene escape and a glimpse into the village's religious heritage.

Vernazza's Beach and Harbour

Vernazza's quaint beach and charming harbour are central to the village's allure. The beach is a delightful spot to unwind, while the harbour provides a picturesque setting with colourful boats lining the waterfront, creating a postcard-perfect scene.

Riomaggiore's Castello (Castle) and Church of San Giovanni Battista

Perched atop a rocky promontory, Riomaggiore's Castello (Castle) offers panoramic views of the village and the Mediterranean. The nearby Church of San Giovanni Battista, with its striking facade, is a landmark that dates back to the 14th century, displaying a blend of Gothic and Genoese styles.

Embark on a journey through the captivating landmarks of Cinque Terre and each step will unveil a new chapter in the rich tapestry of history, culture and natural beauty that defines these coastal villages.

Coastal Kitchen: Sampling Cinque Terre's Culinary Symphony

Cinque Terre not only captivates with its stunning landscapes but also offers a gastronomic journey that celebrates the rich flavours of the Ligurian coast. The region's cuisine is a delightful marriage of fresh seafood, aromatic herbs and local produce, creating a symphony of tastes that reflect the vibrant coastal life. As you explore the five enchanting villages, indulge your senses in the culinary treasures that make Cinque Terre a haven for food enthusiasts. From traditional seafood dishes to savoury pastas, each culinary delight is a homage to the region's maritime heritage and agricultural bounty.

Acciughe Marinate

Acciughe Marinate showcases the simplicity and elegance of Cinque Terre's seafood fare. Fresh anchovies are marinated in a blend of vinegar, garlic and herbs, resulting in a flavourful and tangy appetizer. Served on crusty bread or as part of a seafood antipasto, marinated anchovies offer a taste of the sea with each bite.

Capon Magro

Capon Magro is a culinary masterpiece that originated in Liguria. This elaborate seafood salad features layers of poached fish, shellfish and vegetables, adorned with a vibrant green sauce. The dish is a feast for the eyes and palate, showcasing the artistry of Ligurian cuisine.

Linguine ai Frutti di Mare

Indulge in the bounty of the sea with Linguine ai Frutti di Mare, a seafood pasta dish that features linguine tossed with an assortment of fresh shellfish, clams and squid. Seasoned with garlic, parsley and a touch of white wine, this dish is a seafood lover's dream.

Pesto alla Genovese

A crown jewel of Ligurian cuisine, Pesto alla Genovese is a vibrant green sauce made from fresh basil, pine nuts, garlic, Parmesan cheese and extra-virgin olive oil. Often paired with trofie pasta or drizzled over bruschetta, this aromatic sauce is a quintessential representation of Cinque Terre's commitment to using the finest local ingredients.

Savoury Focaccia

Cinque Terre's Savoury Focaccia is a culinary masterpiece that elevates this simple bread into a flavourful delight. Topped with a medley of ingredients such as olives, cherry tomatoes and aromatic herbs, the focaccia is both a snack and a versatile accompaniment to local meals.

Sciacchetra

Sciacchetrà is a sweet wine that hails from the terraced vineyards of Cinque Terre. Crafted from sun-dried grapes, this amber-coloured dessert wine offers a perfect balance of sweetness and complexity. Sip on Sciacchetra as you toast to the flavours of Cinque Terre and the richness of its culinary heritage.

Farinata

Farinata is a savoury chickpea pancake that reflects the region's rustic and hearty fare. Made with chickpea flour, water and olive oil, farinata is baked until golden brown, resulting in a crispy exterior and a tender interior. Often enjoyed as a street food snack, farinata is a flavourful and satisfying treat.

Embark on a culinary odyssey through Cinque Terre, where each dish narrates a story of maritime traditions, agricultural bounty and the sheer joy of savouring life on the Italian Riviera.

Enigmatic enclaves: Unveiling Cinque Terre's secret treasures

As you traverse the vibrant coastal villages of Cinque Terre, known for their colourful houses, dramatic cliffs and crystalline waters, it's the hidden gems that add a layer of intrigue to the narrative. Beyond the well-trodden paths, these enigmatic treasures are tucked away, waiting to be discovered by the discerning traveller. From secret viewpoints offering panoramic vistas to tucked-away chapels with centuries-old stories, Cinque Terre's hidden gems invite you to explore the lesser-known facets of this Italian Riviera paradise. Embark on a journey of discovery as we unveil these captivating and often overlooked jewels that contribute to the timeless allure of Cinque Terre.

Sanctuary of Soviore

High above Monterosso, the Sanctuary of Soviore is a hidden gem steeped in history. Dating back to the 13th century, this remote hilltop sanctuary offers breath-taking views of the coastline and a peaceful escape from the more touristy areas below. The journey to Soviore is an adventure itself, with a scenic trail leading through lush olive groves and ancient stone steps.

The Underground Wine Press in Vernazza

Explore Vernazza's hidden wine culture by discovering the ancient underground wine press. Tucked away beneath the village, this historic cellar showcases the traditional winemaking methods of the region. The cool, dimly lit space offers a fascinating glimpse into Vernazza's viticultural heritage.

Manarola's Nessun Dorma Terrace

While the Nessun Dorma restaurant is well-known, the hidden gem lies in its terrace. Perched on the cliffs, the terrace provides an unparalleled vantage point for witnessing the sun dip below the horizon, casting a golden glow over the village and the sea. It's an intimate spot to enjoy a drink and savour the magical moments of the Cinque Terre sunset.

Secret Beach in Monterosso

Escape the bustling crowds and discover Monterosso's secret beach, a secluded cove nestled between rugged cliffs. Accessed through a hidden trail, this intimate stretch of sand offers tranquillity and unobstructed views of the Ligurian Sea, providing a serene retreat for those seeking a more secluded coastal experience.

Manarola's Seafront Grotto

Embark on a coastal adventure to discover Manarola's seafront grotto, a natural cave tucked beneath the colourful houses. With the waves gently lapping at its entrance, this hidden enclave provides a unique perspective of the village and an opportunity to immerse yourself in the rhythmic sounds of the sea.

Vernazza's Wine Tasting Terrace

Escape the bustling piazza in Vernazza and discover a hidden terrace for wine tasting. With a selection of local wines and a backdrop of the village and sea, this tranquil spot offers a relaxed atmosphere to savour the flavours of Cinque Terre while avoiding the crowds.

Corniglia's Sunset Terrace

Cap off your day with Corniglia's hidden sunset terrace, a secluded perch overlooking the Mediterranean. Away from the bustling viewpoints, this tranquil spot offers a front-row seat to the spectacular hues of the setting sun, casting a warm glow over the terraced landscapes of Cinque Terre.

Manarola's Love Windows

Discover Manarola's charming 'Love Windows', a series of heart-shaped windows that adorn the facades of houses along the main street. This hidden gem adds a whimsical touch to the village, inviting visitors to search for these romantic details while exploring the colourful alleys and capturing unique moments against the backdrop of the Ligurian architecture.

Embark on a journey of exploration as you unveil the hidden gems of Cinque Terre, each one adding a layer of mystery and enchantment to the captivating tapestry of this coastal paradise.

Trailblazing tales: Outdoor pursuits in Cinque Terre's scenic landscapes

Cinque Terre, with its rugged cliffs, azure waters and charming villages, beckons adventurers to explore its outdoor wonders. Beyond the colourful facades and lively streets, the Italian Riviera offers a playground for outdoor enthusiasts. From exhilarating hikes along the coastal trails to water-based escapades that reveal hidden coves, Cinque Terre invites you to immerse yourself in the natural beauty of this UNESCO World Heritage site. Let us uncover a plethora of outdoor activities that promise not only breath-taking views but also an intimate connection with the coastal landscapes and pristine waters of Cinque Terre.

Cinque Terre coastal trail

Embark on the iconic Cinque Terre Coastal Trail, a series of interconnected paths that weave through the villages and offer panoramic views of the Ligurian Sea. Each segment of the trail unveils a new perspective, from the terraced vineyards of Manarola to the dramatic cliffs of Vernazza, creating a hiking experience that captures the essence of Cinque Terre's coastal beauty.

Kayaking in Monterosso Bay

Paddle through the crystalline waters of Monterosso Bay on a kayaking adventure. Explore hidden coves, glide past sea cliffs and witness the villages from a unique vantage point. Kayaking in Cinque Terre provides an intimate connection with the maritime landscapes and an opportunity to discover secluded spots inaccessible by land.

Riomaggiore to Manarola Via Dell'Amore walk

Embark on the romantic Via Dell'Amore walk, a short but enchanting trail that connects Riomaggiore and Manarola. As you stroll along the cliffside path, take in breath-taking views of the sea, leaving love locks along the way. This leisurely walk is perfect for those seeking a romantic and picturesque outdoor experience.

Snorkelling in Vernazza

Dive into the underwater wonders of Vernazza by snorkelling along its coastline. The clear waters reveal vibrant marine life, hidden rock formations and the unique seafloor beneath. Snorkelling provides a refreshing and immersive way to appreciate the natural beauty that extends from the shores to the depths of the Ligurian Sea.

Corniglia to Manarola scenic train ride

Enjoy a scenic train ride from Corniglia to Manarola, a unique outdoor experience that offers stunning vistas of the coastline. The short journey provides a leisurely way to appreciate the beauty of Cinque Terre's landscapes while enjoying the convenience of the coastal train network.

Rock climbing in Riomaggiore

Challenge your adventurous spirit with rock climbing in Riomaggiore. The rugged cliffs that define the landscape provide an ideal setting for climbers of various skill levels. Whether you're a seasoned climber or a beginner seeking a thrilling introduction to the sport, Riomaggiore's rocky terrain promises an exhilarating experience.

Monterosso's beach volleyball

Bask in the sun and enjoy a game of beach volleyball on Monterosso's golden sands. The lively atmosphere and stunning coastal backdrop create the perfect setting for friendly matches or simply lounging by the sea. Monterosso's expansive beach offers a blend of relaxation and outdoor recreation.

Diving in Vernazza's underwater reserve

Dive into the marine wonders of Vernazza's Underwater Reserve, a protected area rich in biodiversity. Scuba diving allows you to explore vibrant reefs, encounter colourful marine life and witness the fascinating underwater ecosystems that thrive along the Cinque Terre coastline.

Cinque Terre sailing Eexcursion
Sail along the coast of Cinque Terre on a guided excursion that unveils the villages from the sea. With the wind in your sails, discover hidden coves, secluded beaches and the picturesque landscapes of the Italian Riviera. A sailing adventure offers a tranquil and intimate experience with the coastal charm of Cinque Terre.

Vernazza's sunset yoga on the rocks

Immerse yourself in the serenity of Vernazza's sunset yoga on the rocks. With the sea as your backdrop and the sun setting over the horizon, this outdoor yoga experience creates a harmonious blend of relaxation and nature. Join a session to rejuvenate both body and spirit amidst the coastal beauty.

Climbing to Corniglia's Santa Maria sanctuary

Embark on a scenic climb to Corniglia's Santa Maria Sanctuary, perched on a hilltop overlooking the sea. The ascent offers not only a physical challenge but also rewards you with breath-taking panoramic views of the coastline. This outdoor activity combines fitness with cultural exploration.

Vernazza's coastal photography workshop

Hone your photography skills with a coastal photography workshop in Vernazza. Led by a local expert, explore the best vantage points for capturing the beauty of the villages, cliffs and seascapes. This outdoor activity combines artistic expression with the breath-taking scenery of Cinque Terre.

Cinque Terre carnivals: A colourful showcase of local traditions

Immerse yourself in the rich cultural tapestry of Cinque Terre, where time-honoured traditions and vibrant festivals celebrate the spirit of this coastal haven. From centuries-old rituals to lively events that bring the villages to life, Cinque Terre's local traditions and festivals offer a glimpse into the heart of the communities that thrive along the Italian Riviera. Come along with me as we discover the diverse array of cultural expressions that contribute to the unique identity of each village, adding a layer of depth to the enchanting landscapes of Cinque Terre.

Feast of the Assumption in Monterosso (August)

Celebrate the Feast of the Assumption in Monterosso, a religious festival that honours the Virgin Mary. The village comes alive with processions, colourful decorations and a vibrant atmosphere. Pilgrims and locals alike gather to participate in the religious events, culminating in a breath-taking display of fireworks over the Ligurian Sea.

Corniglia's Wine Harvest Festival (September)

Partake in Corniglia's Wine Harvest Festival, a celebration of the region's winemaking heritage. As the grape harvest commences, the village comes alive with grape-stomping competitions, traditional music and, of course, ample opportunities to savour locally produced wines. It's a festive occasion that captures the essence of Cinque Terre's viticultural traditions.

Riomaggiore's Festival of San Giovanni (June)

Join Riomaggiore's Festival of San Giovanni, an annual event honouring the patron saint of the village. Festivities include religious processions, live music and a lively street fair. The air is filled with the aromas of traditional Ligurian cuisine, creating a joyful and communal atmosphere.

Cinque Terre's Maritime Procession (August)

Experience the Maritime Procession that unites the villages of Cinque Terre in a display of maritime solidarity. Decorated boats, each representing a different village, parade along the coast, symbolizing the interconnectedness of these coastal communities.

Manarola's Nativity Scene on the Water (December)

Experience the magic of Manarola's Nativity Scene on the Water, a unique tradition that transforms the village into a living nativity scene. Handcrafted boats adorned with illuminated figures depict the story of Christmas, creating a mesmerizing spectacle against the backdrop of the sea.

Corniglia's Procession of the Cross (April)

Join Corniglia's Procession of the Cross, a solemn religious tradition that takes place during Holy Week. Pilgrims and locals participate in a candlelit procession through the village, reflecting on the significance of Easter and embracing the spiritual essence of the season.

Vernazza's Festival of Santa Margherita (July)

Celebrate the Festival of Santa Margherita in Vernazza, dedicated to the patron saint of the village. The festivities include religious processions, lively music performances and a joyful gathering of locals and visitors. It's a time to pay homage to the village's protective saint and revel in the spirit of community.

Cinque Terre's Chestnut Festival (October)

Indulge in the earthy flavours of the Chestnut Festival that sweeps through Cinque Terre during autumn. Villages, including Monterosso and Riomaggiore, host events highlighting the versatility of chestnuts, from roasted delights to chestnut-infused dishes, capturing the essence of the fall season.

Coastal chronicles: Navigating Cinque Terre's charms with insider finesse

Embarking on a journey to the enchanting coastal villages of Cinque Terre is a venture into a world of vibrant colours, breath-taking landscapes and timeless charm. To ensure your exploration of this UNESCO World Heritage site is as seamless as it is memorable, here are indispensable travel tips that will guide you through the maze of cobblestone streets, scenic trails and coastal wonders. From the best ways to traverse the villages to insider insights on local customs, let these travel tips enhance your Cinque Terre adventure, making it a truly unforgettable experience.

Purchase the Cinque Terre card

Opt for the Cinque Terre Card, a comprehensive pass that grants you access to the national park's trails, shuttle buses and public Wi-Fi. Available for various durations, this card simplifies your exploration and supports the maintenance of the park's natural beauty.

Visit during shoulder seasons

Plan your visit during the shoulder seasons of spring (April to June) or fall (September to October). These months offer pleasant weather, fewer crowds and the opportunity to witness the villages in full bloom or adorned with autumn hues.

Comfortable footwear for hiking

Pack sturdy and comfortable footwear, especially if you plan to explore the scenic hiking trails connecting the villages. The trails vary in difficulty, so having reliable shoes ensures a comfortable and enjoyable trek.

Learn basic Italian phrases

While English is widely spoken, learning a few basic Italian phrases can enhance your interactions with locals and add a personal touch to your experience. Grazie (thank you) and Buongiorno (good morning) go a long way.

Cash is king

Many local establishments may prefer cash transactions, so it's advisable to carry some euros. While larger towns have ATMs, having cash on hand can be convenient, especially in the more secluded areas.

Stay hydrated and protect your skin

Given the sunny climate, stay hydrated during your explorations. Carry a reusable water bottle and apply sunscreen, as you'll likely spend a significant amount of time outdoors.

Mind the train schedules

Familiarize yourself with the train schedules connecting the Cinque Terre villages. Trains are a convenient mode of transportation between the villages and neighbouring towns. Be sure to check the schedules, especially if you plan on making multiple stops.

Be mindful of trail closures

Check for trail closures and maintenance updates before embarking on any hikes. Due to preservation efforts, some trails may be temporarily closed. Stay informed to avoid disappointment and plan alternative routes.

Embrace the slow pace

Cinque Terre embodies a slow-paced lifestyle, so embrace it. Allow yourself time to savour the views, engage with locals and relish the simple pleasures of each village. Rushing through defeats the purpose of experiencing the true essence of Cinque Terre.

Pack a day bag for explorations

Pack a day bag with essentials like water, sunscreen, a map and snacks for your explorations. Whether hiking, exploring villages, or lounging by the sea, having a well-equipped bag ensures a comfortable and prepared journey.

Respect local customs

Respect the local customs and traditions. Whether it's maintaining a quiet demeanour during siesta hours or dressing modestly when visiting religious sites, being culturally sensitive enhances your connection with the local way of life.

Stay flexible with plans

While planning is essential, allow for flexibility in your itinerary. Weather conditions or unexpected discoveries may lead you to alter your plans and being open to spontaneity often leads to the most memorable experiences.

Utilize the shuttle services

Take advantage of the local shuttle services that connect some of the villages. It's a convenient way to hop between locations without the need for extensive walking, especially if you're pressed for time.

Capture sunset moments

Make it a point to capture the mesmerizing sunset moments in Cinque Terre. Each village offers unique vantage points and the warm hues reflecting off the sea create unforgettable memories.

Clifftop gem: Concluding the Cinque Terre odyssey with coastal whispers

As one navigates through the pages of this exploration into the enchanting world of Cinque Terre, it is impossible not to be captivated by the seamless fusion of history, natural beauty and vibrant local culture that defines this coastal gem.

The five villages, perched on the cliffs of the Italian Riviera, beckon travellers with their kaleidoscopic hues, ancient alleyways and panoramic views of the Ligurian Sea. From the medieval origins shaped by maritime trade and the need for protection to the present-day tapestry woven with the threads of communal spirit, Cinque Terre stands as a living testament to the resilience and adaptability of its people.

Burano: A palette of colours on Venetian canals

Jay Chandarana

Venetian palette: A prelude to Burano's enchanted colours

As you venture into the heart of the Venetian Lagoon, the vibrant hues of Burano paint a captivating canvas that beckons you into a world of unparalleled charm. Renowned for its kaleidoscopic facades, Burano stands as a living testament to the artistic spirit of the Venetian archipelago. Burano, a charming island in the Venetian Lagoon, lies approximately 40 minutes by boat from Venice. Burano is situated at a relatively low altitude. The highest point on the island is only a few meters above sea level, making it susceptible to flooding during high tides. Each house, adorned in brilliant shades of red, blue, yellow and green, creates a symphony of colours that dances in harmony with the shimmering canals. This introduction unveils Burano as a gem of the Venetian Isles, where every cobblestone street and picturesque bridge leads to a story woven into the fabric of its vibrant community.

Beyond its renowned colours, Burano is celebrated for its rich artisanal traditions, notably lace-making-an art passed down through generations. As you navigate the narrow alleys, you will encounter centuries-old craftsmanship and a cultural tapestry that transcends time. The leaning bell tower of San Martino stands sentinel over the island, inviting you to explore a destination where every step is a brushstroke and every corner reveals a masterpiece in the grand tableau of Venetian allure. Welcome to Burano, a vivacious chapter in the story of Venice, where artistry, colour and heritage converge in a harmonious blend along the picturesque canals of the lagoon.

Pastel chronicles: Burano's time-weathered heritage

Burano, beyond its kaleidoscopic facades, holds a profound historical significance deeply intertwined with the rich tapestry of Venetian heritage. The origins of this captivating island trace back to Roman times, evolving into a fishing community during the Middle Ages. The historical narrative of Burano is narrated through its charming streets and centuries-old buildings, revealing a story shaped by maritime endeavours and artisanal craftsmanship. The leaning bell tower of San Martino, dating back to the 16th century, stands as a sentinel to Burano's historical journey, offering panoramic views of the lagoon and serving as a testament to the island's enduring legacy.

Burano's historical significance is further enriched by its role as a hub for lace-making- a tradition dating back to the 16th century. The island's lace artisans, known for their meticulous craftsmanship, contributed to the flourishing trade of Venetian lace, making Burano synonymous with this delicate art form. As you wander through the lively squares and pastel-hued streets, each step unveils layers of history, showcasing Burano as not just a picturesque outpost but a living testament to the resilience and cultural richness that define the Venetian archipelago

Vibrant canals: Embarking on Burano's artistic journey

Burano's local culture is a vibrant symphony that harmonizes with the vivid hues of its iconic facades. The island, revered for its artistic spirit, encapsulates the essence of Venetian creativity. Beyond the meticulously painted houses, the locals of Burano are stewards of an age-old tradition-lace-making. Passed down through generations, the art of Burano lace is not merely a craft; it's a cultural emblem that resonates with the island's identity. As you navigate the narrow streets, you'll encounter artisanal workshops where skilled hands meticulously weave intricate lace patterns, showcasing a dedication to heritage that defines Burano's cultural landscape.

Culinary traditions in Burano further immerse visitors in the local way of life. The island's seafood-centric cuisine invites you to savour the flavours of the lagoon, with fresh catches prepared in traditional Venetian style. Small family-run trattorias line the canals, providing not just a culinary experience but a glimpse into the warmth and conviviality that characterize Burano's local hospitality. From the artistic endeavours of lace-makers to the conviviality of shared meals, Burano's local culture unfolds as a tapestry of creativity, craftsmanship and genuine camaraderie that invites you to become a part of its living story.

Colourful canals: Discovering Burano's enchanting charms

Nestled in the Venetian Lagoon, Burano emerges as a kaleidoscope of colours and a haven of Venetian charm. Renowned for its vibrant, candy-coloured houses and lively canals, Burano beckons travellers to discover its unique landmarks that embody the spirit of this picturesque island. From iconic leaning towers to centuries-old churches, each landmark in Burano contributes to the island's distinctive character. Join us on an enchanting journey through Burano's landmarks, where every corner tells a tale of history, tradition and the enduring allure of this Venetian gem.

Tre Ponti

Tre Ponti, or Three Bridges, is a picturesque canal crossing that provides a stunning view of Burano's colourful houses. It's a favourite spot for photographers and artists, offering a composition of vibrant reflections and Venetian charm. The bridges connect different parts of the island, adding to Burano's enchanting atmosphere.

Via Baldassarre Galuppi

Named after the renowned Venetian composer Baldassarre Galuppi, this charming street is a delightful promenade on Burano. Lined with colourful houses and small shops, Via Baldassarre Galuppi exudes a lively atmosphere. It's the perfect place for a leisurely stroll, offering glimpses of daily life on the island.

Museo del Merletto (Lace Museum)

Burano is famed for its centuries-old tradition of lace-making and the Museo del Merletto showcases this exquisite craft. Housed in a beautiful palace, the museum displays delicate lace artifacts, tools and historical pieces that provide insight into Burano's lace-making heritage.

Leaning Bell Tower of San Martino

The Leaning Bell Tower of San Martino, reminiscent of Pisa's famous tower, is one of Burano's most iconic landmarks. Located near the Church of San Martino, the tower's charming tilt adds character to the island's skyline. Climb to the top for panoramic views of Burano's vibrant rooftops and the surrounding lagoon.

Church of San Martino

Adjacent to the leaning bell tower, the Church of San Martino is a centuries-old religious site with roots dating back to the 16th century. The church's interior is adorned with beautiful artworks, including paintings by Venetian masters, making it a cultural and spiritual centrepiece for locals and visitors alike.

Campo Baldassarre Galuppi

Campo Baldassarre Galuppi, the main square of Burano, is a lively hub surrounded by colourful houses, cafes and shops. Named after the Venetian composer, the square is a central gathering point for locals and visitors. It's an ideal spot to savour the island's atmosphere and indulge in local delicacies.

Isola di San Francesco del Deserto

While technically not on Burano itself, the nearby Isola di San Francesco del Deserto is a small island that can be reached by boat. Home to a Franciscan monastery, lush gardens and a tranquil atmosphere, this hidden gem offers a peaceful escape from the vibrant bustle of Burano.

Scalzi Bridge

Connecting Burano with Mazzorbo, the Scalzi Bridge is a charming wooden footbridge that spans a narrow canal. This picturesque bridge allows visitors to traverse the islands and absorb the serene beauty of the lagoon. It's simple yet elegant design complements the timeless allure of Burano.

Burano's landmarks weave together a tapestry of history, art and the unique spirit of Venetian Island life. As you explore each colourful corner and cross its charming bridges, Burano invites you to step into a world where tradition meets vibrant creativity in the heart of the Venetian Lagoon.

Artisanal flavours: Indulging in Burano's culinary creations

Beyond the vibrant facades and enchanting canals of Burano lies a culinary haven that beckons all those who appreciate the artistry of flavours. Bursting with the warmth of Venetian hospitality, Burano's culinary scene is as diverse and colourful as its iconic houses. From seafood treasures to delectable pastries, each dish is a celebration of the island's rich traditions and the bounties of the surrounding lagoon. Let us embark on a gastronomic journey through the delightful culinary delights that make Burano a destination for the senses.

Risotto al Nero di Seppia

A masterpiece of Venetian cuisine, Risotto al Nero di Seppia is a savoury delight that captures the essence of Burano's seafood culture. Prepared with cuttlefish ink, the risotto takes on a rich, ebony hue and is infused with the briny flavours of the lagoon. Served with fresh seafood, it's a culinary symphony that transports diners to the heart of the Venetian culinary tradition.

Bussolà Buranello

Indulge your sweet tooth with Bussolà Buranello, a traditional Venetian butter biscuit that is a signature treat of Burano. Shaped like a ring or an 'S', these crumbly delights are often enjoyed with a cup of coffee or dipped into sweet wine. The subtle buttery taste and delicate texture make them a beloved sweet companion for locals and visitors alike.

Grisoli

Grisoli are delicate pastries that originate from the Venetian tradition. These fried dough strips are sprinkled with powdered sugar, creating a delightful contrast between the crispiness of the pastry and the sweetness of the sugar. Grisoli are often enjoyed during festive occasions and celebrations on the island.

Branzino all'Isolana

Branzino all'Isolana is a sumptuous seafood dish that exemplifies the flavours of the lagoon. Sea bass is expertly prepared with local herbs and olive oil, capturing the essence of Burano's maritime heritage. Served with a side of fresh vegetables, it's a culinary masterpiece that highlights the pristine ingredients available in the surrounding waters.

Risotto de Go

Another risotto delicacy that graces the tables of Burano is Risotto de Go, featuring the flavours of the lagoon's most prized shellfish, the go. This rice dish, expertly cooked to creamy perfection, showcases the natural sweetness and tenderness of the go, offering a taste of the sea in every spoonful.

Sarde in Saor

Sarde in Saor is a traditional Venetian dish that finds its way to Burano's culinary repertoire. This sweet and sour delicacy features marinated sardines, typically flavoured with onions, pine nuts and raisins. The combination of savoury and sweet notes creates a harmonious dish that reflects the influence of Venetian trade history.

Polenta e Schie

Polenta e Schie is a dish that combines the rustic goodness of polenta with the delicate flavours of tiny shrimp known as 'schie'. The shrimp are often sautéed with garlic and parsley, creating a savoury topping for the creamy polenta. This dish showcases the connection between Burano's culinary offerings and the bounty of the Venetian Lagoon.

Linguine alle Vongole

Linguine alle Vongole is a classic seafood pasta dish that graces the tables of Burano. Fresh clams are sautéed with garlic, white wine and a hint of chili, creating a delectable sauce that coats the perfectly cooked linguine. This dish embodies the simplicity and elegance of Venetian cuisine.

Burano's culinary landscape is a mosaic of flavours, where each dish is crafted with care and a deep connection to the island's history. From the savoury depths of seafood risottos to the sweet pleasures of pastries, the culinary delights of Burano invite you to savour the essence of Venetian gastronomy amidst a backdrop of vivid hues.

Whispers of the lagoon: Discovering Burano's hidden wonders

Beyond the iconic canals and vibrant facades that define Burano's postcard-perfect charm, lies a realm of hidden gems waiting to be discovered. These lesser-known treasures reveal a side of Burano that goes beyond the well-trodden paths, offering a glimpse into the island's secrets and surprises. Join me on an exploration of Burano's hidden gems, where quiet alleyways, local artisans and charming corners await those seeking a more intimate connection with this Venetian jewel.

Fondamenta degli Assassini

Fondamenta degli Assassini is a narrow waterfront path that unveils a quieter side of Burano. Away from the bustling crowds, this hidden gem offers a peaceful stroll along the canals, where local life unfolds at its own pace. The name, with its mysterious connotations, adds an intriguing allure to this lesser-known corner.

San Mauro church

San Mauro Church is a hidden architectural gem, often overlooked by visitors. Tucked away in a quieter part of Burano, this charming church boasts a beautiful facade and an intimate interior adorned with religious art. The serene atmosphere makes it a perfect retreat for those seeking moments of contemplation.

Gioielleria Eredi Jovon

For those seeking unique treasures, Gioielleria Eredi Jovon is a hidden gem of a jewellery store with a rich history. Located on Via Baldassarre Galuppi, this family-owned shop has been crafting exquisite jewellery for generations. Visitors can explore a collection of handmade pieces, each reflecting the artistry of Venetian craftsmanship.

Libreria Acqua Alta

Nestled in the heart of Burano, Libreria Acqua Alta is a unique and quirky bookstore that captures the imagination. Known for its 'book stairs' made of gondolas and a courtyard filled with books piled in bathtubs, this hidden gem celebrates the whimsical spirit of Burano. Bibliophiles and curious souls will find this literary haven a delightful surprise.

Campo Barbaro

Campo Barbaro is a charming square that radiates a serene ambiance, offering respite from the more crowded areas of Burano. Surrounded by colourful houses and the Church of San Pietro Martire, this hidden gem provides a tranquil space for visitors to relax and soak in the local atmosphere.

Riva di San Martino

Riva di San Martino is a charming waterfront stretch that remains off the beaten path. Away from the more touristy areas, this hidden gem offers a peaceful ambience, where visitors can admire the reflections of colourful houses in the tranquil waters of the canal. It's a serene spot to enjoy the unique beauty of Burano.

Scuola Grande di San Mauro

The Scuola Grande di San Mauro is a hidden architectural gem that showcases the grandeur of Venetian Gothic design. While not as famous as some other landmarks, this former confraternity building boasts intricate details on its facade. Visitors can appreciate the historical and artistic significance of this hidden treasure.

Burano's hidden gems unveil a side of the island that goes beyond its famous canals and brightly painted facades. Exploring these lesser-known corners allows visitors to discover the authentic charm, local stories and timeless beauty that make Burano a truly enchanting destination.

Canal-side adventures: Outdoor exploration in Burano's colourful setting

Burano, with its kaleidoscope of colourful houses and meandering canals, is not only a feast for the eyes but also a haven for outdoor enthusiasts seeking to immerse themselves in nature's embrace. Beyond the charming streets, the island offers a variety of outdoor activities that allow visitors to explore the unique landscapes of the Venetian Lagoon. From leisurely strolls along the waterfront to exciting excursions on the water, Burano beckons those who yearn for open skies and the invigorating scent of the sea. Come along with me as we discover the outdoor wonders of Burano, where every step and paddle stroke unveil a new facet of this enchanting island.

Canal-side stroll along Fondamenta Pontinello

Begin your outdoor adventure with a leisurely stroll along Fondamenta Pontinello, a charming canal-side promenade. Lined with vibrant houses, this picturesque path offers a perfect introduction to the unique architecture and tranquil atmosphere of Burano. As you walk, take in the reflections of the colourful facades dancing on the water's surface.

Explore the Lido di Burano beach

For those seeking a sun-soaked escape, the Lido di Burano Beach awaits. Just a short waterbus ride away, this pristine stretch of sand offers a retreat from the bustle of the main island. Relax on the shores, feel the gentle lagoon breeze and savour the panoramic views of Burano's skyline.

Kayaking in the Venetian lagoon

Embark on a kayaking adventure to discover the hidden corners of the Venetian Lagoon surrounding Burano. Paddle through narrow channels, pass by traditional fishing huts and marvel at the natural beauty that unfolds as you explore the lagoon at your own pace. Kayaking provides a unique perspective of Burano's landscape from the water.

Bird watching at the Torcello marshes

Nature enthusiasts will delight in the bird-watching opportunities at the Torcello Marshes, a short boat ride from Burano. This protected natural area is home to a variety of bird species, including herons, cormorants and flamingos. Bring your binoculars and immerse yourself in the peaceful serenity of this birdwatcher's paradise.

Bicycle tour of Burano and Mazzorbo

Rent a bicycle and explore the charming islands of Burano and Mazzorbo on two wheels. Cruise along narrow paths, cross picturesque bridges and discover the quieter corners of the lagoon. This cycling adventure offers a delightful blend of exploration and a touch of local life.

Sunset cruise in a traditional Bragozzo

Experience the magic of a Venetian sunset with a cruise aboard a traditional bragozzo. These historic fishing boats have been repurposed for leisure, providing an intimate and romantic setting. As the sun dips below the horizon, the tranquil waters of the lagoon transform into a canvas of warm hues.

Photography expedition to Piazza Baldassarre Galuppi

Calling all photographers! Capture the essence of Burano's outdoor charm in the iconic Piazza Baldassarre Galuppi. Known as the 'Composer's Square', this lively gathering place is adorned with vibrant houses and local cafes. Find the perfect angle to frame the vivid colours and energetic atmosphere of this central square.

Sailing excursion to the Mazzorbetto Islands

Embark on a sailing excursion to the Mazzorbetto Islands, a hidden gem in the Venetian Lagoon. Sail through the calm waters, anchor in secluded coves and take a dip in the refreshing lagoon. This sailing adventure provides a serene escape, surrounded by the natural beauty of the lagoon.

Stand-Up Paddleboarding in Burano's canals

For a unique perspective of Burano's canals, try stand-up paddleboarding (SUP). Glide through the narrow waterways, passing beneath charming bridges and alongside vibrant houses. SUP offers a balance of relaxation and adventure as you navigate the labyrinthine canals at your own pace.

Picnic at Parco delle Rimembranze

Escape to Parco delle Rimembranze for a delightful picnic amidst nature. This waterfront park provides a tranquil setting with shaded areas and panoramic views. Pack a basket with local delicacies, unwind on the grass and savour the serene ambiance of this green oasis.

Rowing Lesson in a Venetian gondola

Experience the art of Venetian rowing with a lesson in a traditional gondola. Skilled instructors will guide you through the techniques, allowing you to navigate the canals with finesse. This hands-on activity provides a deeper appreciation for the craftsmanship and skill involved in the iconic gondola.

Lighthouse visit at Faro di Murano

For panoramic views of the lagoon, take a boat to Faro di Murano, the lighthouse that guards the entrance to the Venetian Lagoon. Climb to the top for breath-taking vistas of Burano, the surrounding islands and the vast expanse of the lagoon. It's a unique vantage point that rewards the adventurous spirit.

Art in the open: Street painting festival

If you're lucky to visit during the Street Painting Festival, immerse yourself in the outdoor art scene. Watch as local and international artists transform Burano's streets into vibrant canvases, creating temporary masterpieces that add a burst of colour to the island's outdoor landscape.

Burano's outdoor activities offer a diverse range of experiences, allowing visitors to connect with nature, adventure and the unique charm of the Venetian Lagoon. Whether strolling along canals, sailing into the sunset, or exploring hidden corners, each outdoor adventure in Burano promises a memorable journey under the open skies.

Island extravaganza: Burano's vibrant celebration of local traditions

Burano, the vibrant jewel of the Venetian Lagoon, is not only a visual feast for its kaleidoscope of painted houses but also a cultural treasure trove brimming with local traditions and lively festivals. Beyond its charming canals and bustling squares, the island comes alive with celebrations that reflect the spirit of its community. Let us delve into the rich tapestry of Burano's local traditions and festivals, where each event unveils a unique aspect of the island's cultural identity. From centuries-old rituals to modern-day revelries, Burano's festivities offer a glimpse into the heart and soul of this enchanting Venetian gem.

Festa di San Martino (November)

The island of Burano celebrates the Festa di San Martino, honouring Saint Martin. This traditional feast includes a procession through the streets, led by the statue of the saint. Locals and visitors alike join in the festivities, enjoying music, dance and a vibrant market offering local delicacies. The highlight is the blessing of the new wine, symbolizing the arrival of autumn.

Festa di San Pietro Martire (April)

San Pietro Martire, the patron saint of Burano, is honoured in a grand celebration. The festivities include a religious procession, during which the statue of the saint is carried through the streets. The day is marked by religious ceremonies, traditional music performances and a lively atmosphere as the community comes together to celebrate its patron saint.

Festa della Sensa (May)

Burano joins Venice in celebrating the Festa della Sensa, a centuries-old tradition that marks the marriage of the city to the sea. In Burano, the festivities include a boat procession, during which the mayor symbolically drops a ring into the water, symbolizing the union between the community and the sea. The event is a colourful and symbolic expression of maritime heritage.

Notte Rosa (July)

Notte Rosa, or Pink Night, is a modern celebration that has become a highlight on Burano's event calendar. The island bathes in pink lights as shops, houses and public spaces are adorned with pink decorations. The night is filled with music, entertainment and a festive atmosphere that transforms Burano into a magical pink wonderland.

Carnevale di Burano (March)

During the annual Carnevale, Burano transforms into a lively spectacle of colours and costumes. The island's residents, both young and old, don elaborate masks and traditional outfits for a vibrant parade through the streets. The festivities include live music, dancing and a joyful atmosphere that permeates every corner of Burano.

Festa dell'Assunta (August)

The Festa dell'Assunta commemorates the Assumption of Mary and is celebrated with religious processions, church services and a festive ambiance. The day is an important religious event and locals gather to pay homage to the Virgin Mary. The festivities also include cultural performances and traditional music.

Burano in Fiore (April)

Burano in Fiore is a delightful spring festival that celebrates the island's floral beauty. Residents adorn their homes and public spaces with vibrant flower displays, creating a picturesque tapestry of colours. The festival includes flower-themed events, gardening workshops and a lively parade that showcases the island's botanical splendour.

Festa del Redentore (July)

Burano partakes in the citywide celebration of the Festa del Redentore, an event that commemorates the end of the plague in the 16th century. The festivities include spectacular fireworks display over the lagoon, illuminating the night sky and reflecting in the waters surrounding Burano.

Burano Film Festival (September)

For cinephiles and culture enthusiasts, the Burano Film Festival is an annual event that showcases a selection of international and local films. Open-air screenings, film discussions and cultural activities create a vibrant atmosphere as film enthusiasts gather to appreciate cinematic art against the backdrop of Burano's picturesque scenery.

Regata di Burano (September)

The annual Regata di Burano is a thrilling rowing competition that draws participants from neighbouring islands. Locals and visitors gather along the canals to cheer for the skilled rowers as they navigate traditional boats through the challenging course. The regatta is a testament to the island's strong connection to its maritime roots.

Burano's local traditions and festivals weave a tapestry of cultural richness, uniting the island's residents and welcoming visitors into the heart of its vibrant celebrations. Each event reflects the spirit, history and community bonds that make Burano a truly unique and enchanting destination in the Venetian Lagoon.

Beyond the palette: Insider's guide to exploring Burano's delights

Burano, with its whimsical palette of vibrant colours and charming canals, beckons travellers to immerse themselves in its unique tapestry of beauty and culture. As you plan your journey to this Venetian gem, here are invaluable travel tips to ensure a seamless and memorable experience. From navigating the picturesque streets to savouring local delicacies, these tips provide insights that will enhance your stay on this captivating island, making it a journey filled with enchantment and discovery.

Arrive early or stay late

To capture the true essence of Burano without the crowds, consider arriving early in the morning or staying late into the evening. During these hours, the island takes on a serene charm, allowing you to appreciate the vibrant colours and unique architecture in a more intimate setting. Sunrise and sunset offer particularly magical moments for photographers and those seeking a tranquil atmosphere.

Canal-side stroll through Fondamenta Cao di Rio

Escape the main thoroughfares and take a leisurely stroll along Fondamenta Cao di Rio. This canal-side path offers a quieter, more authentic experience, with charming views of the water and traditional houses. Explore the side streets branching off from this promenade to discover hidden gems away from the bustling crowds.

Photography tips for capturing colours

Burano's vibrant colours provide a visual feast, but capturing them requires some photographic finesse. Opt for soft, diffused lighting to enhance the colours and details of the houses. Explore different angles and compositions to showcase the unique character of each building. Early morning or late afternoon light adds a warm glow to your photographs.

Take a Vaporetto ride to Burano

Enhance your arrival experience by taking a vaporetto (water bus) to Burano. The journey offers stunning views of the Venetian Lagoon and allows you to approach the island from the water, showcasing its colourful facades. Choose an outdoor seat on the vaporetto for an unobstructed panorama.

Respect the residents' privacy

While exploring the island's narrow streets, remember that Burano is not just a tourist attraction but a vibrant community. Respect the privacy of residents by refraining from entering private courtyards or photographing inside homes without permission. This consideration ensures a harmonious experience for both visitors and locals.

Explore Mazzorbo

Connected to Burano by a small footbridge, Mazzorbo offers a tranquil contrast to its colourful neighbour. Explore the peaceful vineyards and gardens and visit the 11th-century church of Santa Caterina. Mazzorbo provides a quieter retreat with its own unique charm.

Reserve a table with a canal view

For a memorable dining experience, consider reserving a table at a waterfront restaurant with a canal view. Enjoying a meal against the backdrop of colourful houses and passing boats adds a romantic touch to your culinary adventure. Be sure to book in advance, especially during peak hours.

Use water taxis for convenience

While Burano is a walkable island, utilizing water taxis can be convenient, especially if you have limited time or prefer a quicker mode of transportation. Water taxis offer a scenic way to explore the lagoon and can transport you to neighbouring islands or back to Venice with ease.

Visit Burano's unique churches

Burano is home to several charming churches, each with its own distinctive character. Explore the leaning bell tower of San Martino, the mosaic-adorned façade of San Martino Vescovo and the vibrant interior of the Church of San Francesco del Deserto on nearby Isola San Francesco.

Learn basic Italian phrases

While English is spoken in tourist areas, learning a few basic Italian phrases can enhance your interactions with locals and add a personal touch to your experience. Simple greetings and expressions of gratitude go a long way in fostering a warm connection with the community.

Stay overnight for a tranquil retreat

Consider extending your stay by booking accommodation on Burano. Spending a night on the island provides a peaceful retreat after the day-trippers depart, allowing you to savour the quiet charm and enchantment that define Burano in the evening.

Respect the unique Venetian tides

Keep in mind the influence of tides on Venetian islands, including Burano. Venetian tides can impact water levels, so be prepared for occasional flooding, especially during high tides (aqua alta). Wear appropriate footwear and check the local tide forecast during your visit.

Connect with locals at Piazza Baldassarre Galuppi

Piazza Baldassarre Galuppi, the main square in Burano, is a lively gathering place. Join locals at the cafes, strike up conversations and immerse yourself in the island's social atmosphere. The square offers a vibrant hub where you can absorb the energy of daily life on Burano.

Capture the magic of sunset

Witnessing the sunset over Burano's canals is a magical experience. Find a scenic spot along the waterfront, such as the Fondamenta Pontinello and watch as the sun casts a warm glow on the colourful facades. The changing hues of the sky create a breath-taking backdrop.

Embark on your Burano adventure armed with these travel tips and you'll unlock the secrets of this captivating island. From savouring local flavours to navigating its vibrant streets, each tip is a key to experiencing the true magic of Burano-a place where every alley, every colour and every moment tells a unique story

Burano bliss: Concluding the chapter with radiant musings

As you bid farewell to the wonderland of Burano, the vibrancy of its facades lingers in your heart like a painted memory. This chapter of your Venetian journey, defined by the island's unique culture and artistic flair, concludes with a sense of admiration for the timeless charm etched into every corner.

The cultural symphony, from the delicate artistry of Burano lace to the savoury notes of seafood-infused Venetian cuisine, becomes a cherished melody that accompanies you beyond the lagoon. The legacy of Burano extends beyond its canals and vivid colours-it's a testament to the resilience and creative spirit that defines the essence of Venetian splendour.

Varenna: Lakeside legends unfolded

Lakefront lullaby: A prelude to Varenna's enchanted shores

Nestled on the scenic banks of the Adda River, Varenna welcomes travellers to a Lombardian sanctuary where history and nature intertwine. Varenna, nestled on the eastern shore of Lake Como, is conveniently located just a short ferry ride from the town of Bellagio. As you step into the heart of this charming town, a sense of tranquillity envelops you, accentuated by the soothing murmur of the river and the rustling leaves of ancient trees. Situated at an altitude of approximately 200 meters above sea level, Varenna provides the perfect setting for leisurely strolls along the lakefront promenade and romantic sunsets over the water. Varenna's allure lies not only in its picturesque setting but also in the rich tapestry of Lombardian history woven into its cobbled streets.

This introduction invites you to explore the essence of Varenna, where the medieval architecture reflects the town's storied past. The silhouette of the Church of San Giorgio against the sky, the stone bridges spanning the river and the vibrant markets showcasing local crafts all beckon you to embark on a journey through time. Varenna, with its timeless charm and a backdrop of rolling Lombardian hills, is more than a destination; it's an immersive experience into the cultural and natural treasures that define this Lombardian gem along the Adda River.

Cultural echoes: Varenna's time-honoured narrative

Nestled along the picturesque Adda River, Varenna unfolds as a living testament to Lombardy's rich historical tapestry. The town's roots stretch back to ancient times, evident in the remnants of Roman settlements that dot its landscape. However, it was during the medieval period that Varenna truly came into its own, with the construction of architectural gems that still grace its streets today. Varenna's historical significance is intricately woven into its architectural landscape.

The remnants of Roman dwellings offer glimpses into the town's earliest chapters, while medieval marvels like the Church of San Giorgio and Ponte San Michele stand as testaments to Varenna's enduring spirit. The Church of San Giorgio, with its ancient facade and centuries-old frescoes, encapsulates the religious and artistic fervour that shaped the town's identity. The Ponte San Michele, dating back to medieval times, not only serves as a bridge over the Adda but also symbolizes the continuity of Varenna's heritage. Amidst it all, Villa Gallia, a stately residence, adds a touch of aristocratic elegance to Varenna's narrative. Through these architectural gems, Varenna invites visitors to traverse the corridors of time, immersing themselves in the layers of history that define this enchanting Lombardian town along the Adda River.

Enchanting shores: Unveiling Varenna's lakeside charms

Varenna, while steeped in historical grandeur, also encapsulates a vibrant local culture that harmonizes with the serene rhythms of the Adda River. The town's community cherishes its traditions and this is evident in the lively events and festivals that punctuate the calendar. From the annual Festa di San Giorgio celebrating the town's patron saint to the charming local markets that showcase artisanal crafts and regional delicacies, Varenna invites visitors to partake in its cultural rhapsody.

Varenna's local culture is intricately woven into the fabric of daily life, from the artisanal traditions that shape the town's identity to the culinary delights that tantalize the taste buds. The town's markets, vibrant with colour and energy, showcase local artisans presenting their craft-from handwoven textiles to intricately carved wooden goods. These markets not only provide a platform for local artists but also become communal spaces where residents and visitors converge to celebrate the richness of Varenna's cultural tapestry.

Tranquil treasures: Delving into Varenna's enchanting landmarks

Nestled in the heart of Italy, Varenna is a town that whispers tales of antiquity through its charming streets and cultural treasures. Steeped in history, this hidden gem beckons travellers to explore its landmarks, each revealing a chapter of Varenna's rich heritage. From medieval architecture to religious sanctuaries, the town unfolds a tapestry of historical splendour. Join us on a journey through time as we uncover the captivating landmarks and points of interest that define the allure of Varenna.

Museo Civico di Varenna

For a deeper understanding of Varenna's cultural heritage, visit the Museo Civico di Varenna. Housed in a historic building, the museum showcases artifacts, artworks and archaeological finds that unveil the layers of the town's past. Wander through the exhibits and embark on a journey through Varenna's history.

Piazza del Popolo

Piazza del Popolo serves as the vibrant heart of Varenna, a central square surrounded by historical buildings and lively cafes. The elegant architecture of the Palazzo Comunale and the welcoming atmosphere make it an ideal spot for both leisurely strolls and cultural immersion. The square often hosts local events, adding to its dynamic charm.

Castello di Varenna

Perched atop a hill, the Castello di Varenna offers panoramic views of the surrounding landscape. This medieval fortress, with origins dating to the 11th century, played a crucial role in the town's defence. Explore the well-preserved towers and walls, where each stone whispers stories of Varenna's medieval past.

Basilica di San Pietro

The Basilica di San Pietro stands as a majestic testament to Varenna's religious history. Dating back to the 12th century, this Romanesque gem boasts a harmonious blend of architectural styles. Admire the intricate facade, adorned with sculptures and step inside to discover frescoes, sculptures and the hushed atmosphere of centuries of worship.

Fontana della Piazza

The Fontana della Piazza graces Varenna's central square with its sculpted elegance. This historic fountain, adorned with intricate details, serves as a focal point for locals and visitors alike. Its soothing presence adds a touch of grace to Piazza del Popolo, inviting moments of contemplation amidst the town's bustle.

Oratorio di San Rocco

The Oratorio di San Rocco is a small yet captivating religious sanctuary in Varenna. Admire the frescoes that adorn its interior, depicting scenes from the life of Saint Rocco. This hidden gem offers a tranquil space for reflection, away from the bustling streets of the town.

Varenna's Historic Villas

Embark on a scenic journey to explore Varenna's historic villas, scattered throughout the lush countryside. These noble residences, surrounded by gardens and olive groves, showcase architectural elegance and offer glimpses into the town's aristocratic past. Some, like Villa di Varenna, open their doors to visitors, allowing a peek into a bygone era.

Palazzo Comunale

The Palazzo Comunale, with its stately presence on Piazza del Popolo, is a symbol of Varenna's civic pride. Dating back to the medieval era, the palace has undergone renovations, showcasing a mix of architectural styles. Its facade, adorned with coats of arms, invites visitors to delve into the town's administrative history.

Varenna's landmarks weave a narrative of a town deeply rooted in history, where each stone, square and church tells a story of the passage of time. As you explore these cultural treasures, you'll find yourself immersed in the enchanting legacy of Varenna, a town that wears its history with pride.

Lakefront flavours: Savouring Varenna's culinary serenade

Varenna, a town steeped in history and nestled in the heart of Italy, offers not only architectural marvels but also a delightful journey through its culinary heritage. From age-old recipes passed down through generations to contemporary twists on traditional flavours, Varenna's gastronomic scene is a celebration of regional ingredients and timeless recipes. Come along as we traverse the cobblestone streets, exploring the diverse culinary delights that make Varenna a destination for food enthusiasts seeking a taste of history.

Salame d'Oca

Salame d'Oca, or Goose Salami, is a unique cured meat that showcases Varenna's dedication to preserving age-old culinary practices. Made from goose meat, this salami is seasoned with a blend of spices and air-dried to perfection. Sliced thin, it offers a taste of the town's artisanal craftsmanship.

Torrone Varenna

Satisfy your sweet tooth with Torrone Varenna, a local variation of the classic Italian nougat. This confection combines honey, sugar, egg whites and toasted almonds, resulting in a chewy and nutty treat. Torrone Varenna is often enjoyed during festive occasions, embodying the sweetness of Varenna's traditions.

Bagna Cauda

Experience the warmth and richness of Bagna Cauda, a traditional Piedmontese dish that has found its way into Varenna's kitchens. This 'hot bath' is a communal pot of warm sauce made with garlic, anchovies, olive oil and butter. Dip an array of fresh vegetables into the flavourful concoction, creating a communal and savoury dining experience.

Stracotto d'Asino

For those seeking bold flavours, Stracotto d'Asino is a slow-cooked donkey stew that reflects the agricultural roots of Varenna. The meat is simmered in a robust tomato sauce, wine and aromatic herbs until tender, creating a hearty and rustic dish that harkens back to the town's historic culinary practices.

Formaggio Branzi

Savour the regional cheese, Formaggio Branzi, a semi-hard cheese with a nutty and buttery flavour. Made from cow's milk, this cheese is often enjoyed on its own or incorporated into various dishes. Pair it with local wines for a true taste of Varenna's dairy heritage.

Casoncelli alla Bergamasca

Indulge in the local pasta specialty, Casoncelli alla Bergamasca. These delicate handmade raviolis are filled with a savoury mixture of ground meat, breadcrumbs and aromatic herbs. Served with a drizzle of melted butter and sage, this dish reflects the rustic elegance of Varenna's traditional cuisine.

Crescentina Bergamasca

Crescentina Bergamasca, a type of flatbread, is a staple in Varenna's culinary scene. Often served warm and accompanied by cured meats and cheeses, this simple yet flavourful bread embodies the essence of local craftsmanship and the importance of quality ingredients.

Tiramisu Varenna

Conclude your culinary journey in Varenna with a decadent Tiramisu Varenna. This twist on the classic Italian dessert features layers of espresso-soaked ladyfingers, mascarpone cheese and a dusting of cocoa. The addition of local ingredients imparts a unique flavour that pays homage to the town's culinary identity.

Sbrisolona

Indulge in Sbrisolona, a crumbly almond and cornmeal cake that originated in Lombardy and has become a beloved treat in Varenna. The name 'Sbrisolona' refers to its crumbly texture and the cake is often enjoyed with a drizzle of honey or paired with a glass of Vin Santo.

Polenta e Osei

Polenta e Osei, a dish that originated in Lombardy, holds a special place in Varenna's culinary repertoire. This savoury-sweet delight features polenta paired with small game birds, usually sparrows. The rich and flavourful combination is a testament to the town's connection with the land and its hunting traditions.

In Varenna, each culinary delight is a testament to the town's commitment to preserving its gastronomic legacy. Whether you're savouring pasta dishes that have stood the test of time or exploring contemporary twists on traditional flavours, Varenna's cuisine invites you to partake in a delectable journey through history.

Secrets of the shores: Exploring Varenna's hidden treasures

As you traverse the enchanting streets of Varenna, you'll discover that this town holds secrets and hidden gems waiting to be uncovered. Beyond the well-trodden paths and iconic landmarks, these hidden treasures offer a glimpse into the soul of Varenna, revealing its intimate charm and lesser-known stories. Join me on a journey to explore the hidden gems that add a touch of mystery and allure to the town, inviting you to venture off the beaten path and savour the undiscovered beauty of Varenna.

Ruga dei Misteri

Embark on a journey through time as you stroll along Ruga dei Misteri, a narrow alley that winds its way through the heart of Varenna. Lined with ancient buildings and charming doorways, this hidden passage echoes with whispers of centuries past, inviting you to wander and uncover the mysteries concealed within its cobblestone embrace.

Giardino Segreto

Escape to the Giardino Segreto, or Secret Garden, a hidden oasis where nature and tranquillity converge. Tucked behind ancient stone walls, this verdant sanctuary offers a peaceful respite. Take a leisurely stroll among blooming flowers, manicured hedges and hidden benches-a secret retreat for moments of quiet reflection.

Scala degli Innamorati

Ascend the Scala degli Innamorati, or Lovers' Staircase, a secluded set of steps that winds its way through a quiet neighbourhood. Lined with blooming flowers and quaint doorways, this hidden staircase offers not only a picturesque climb but also a romantic atmosphere that encapsulates the charm of Varenna.

Portico dell'Arte

Step into the Portico dell'Arte, a covered walkway adorned with murals and artistic expressions. This hidden gem serves as a dynamic canvas for local artists, transforming a simple passageway into an outdoor gallery. Wander through this artistic haven, where every step unveils a new perspective on Varenna's creative spirit.

Fountain of Whispers

Seek out the Fountain of Whispers, a hidden fountain tucked away in a quiet courtyard. Surrounded by ancient stone walls, this enchanting spot invites contemplation. Legend has it that if you listen closely, you may catch the echoes of stories whispered by the fountain, adding a touch of magic to this hidden corner.

Teatro dell'Ombra

Enter the Teatro dell'Ombra, a hidden puppet theatre that preserves the tradition of shadow play. Tucked away in a historic building, this intimate venue comes to life with enchanting performances that captivate both young and old. Discover the magic of shadow theatre in this unassuming gem.

Largo dei Libri

Delve into the world of literature at Largo dei Libri, a hidden square that pays homage to the written word. Surrounded by charming bookshops and cosy reading nooks, this literary haven is a sanctuary for book lovers. Uncover rare finds and literary treasures in this tucked-away square.

Antichi Lavatoi

Uncover the Antichi Lavatoi, ancient washhouses hidden along the banks of Varenna's waterways. These centuries-old stone structures once served as communal spaces for

laundry. Now partially overgrown with ivy and surrounded by a sense of nostalgia, these hidden remnants of daily life transport you to a bygone era.

Varenna's hidden gems are like whispered secrets, inviting you to peel back the layers of the town's history and charm. As you explore these lesser-known corners, you'll find that Varenna's true beauty lies not just in its grandeur but in the intimate and hidden spaces that capture the essence of this enchanting Italian town.

Alpine adventures: Embracing outdoor excursions in Varenna's mountainous terrain

Beyond the ancient walls and charming streets of Varenna lies a pristine landscape that beckons outdoor enthusiasts to explore its natural wonders. From invigorating hikes that unveil panoramic views to tranquil waters that mirror the surrounding beauty, Varenna offers a myriad of outdoor activities for those seeking an active escape. Let us embark on a journey through the outdoor adventures that define the enchanting town of Varenna, where every path leads to a discovery and every trail is a step into the embrace of nature.

Monte Varenna trek

Ascend the heights of Monte Varenna on a trek that rewards your efforts with breathtaking vistas. The trail takes you through lush forests, wildflower meadows and rocky outcrops, offering panoramic views of the town below. Reach the summit and marvel at the picturesque landscapes that unfold in every direction.

Cycling along the lakeside

Saddle up for a cycling adventure along the lakeside trails surrounding Varenna. The tranquil roads that hug the shoreline provide a scenic route for cyclists of all levels.

Feel the breeze off the lake as you pedal past olive groves, vineyards and charming villages, soaking in the beauty of the Lombardy countryside.

Kayaking on Lago di Varenna

Explore the pristine waters of Lago di Varenna by kayaking across its serene surface. Glide past ancient villas, hidden coves and waterside gardens as the lake mirrors the beauty of the surrounding hills. Kayaking offers a unique perspective of Varenna, allowing you to connect with the town from the heart of its tranquil waters.

Via Ferrata di Pietra Rossa

For thrill-seekers, the Via Ferrata di Pietra Rossa presents an exhilarating challenge. This rock-climbing route is equipped with iron cables, ladders and bridges that traverse the rugged cliffs of Varenna. Conquer the heights and be rewarded with unparalleled views of the town and its picturesque surroundings.

Fishing by Fiume Serio

Cast your line into the clear waters of Fiume Serio, a river that meanders through the Lombardy region. Fishing enthusiasts can try their luck in catching local species while enjoying the tranquillity of the riverbanks. It's a peaceful and rewarding way to connect with nature in the outskirts of Varenna.

Paragliding over Varenna

Experience the thrill of paragliding as you soar over the landscapes of Varenna. Launch from elevated points and glide through the air, capturing bird's-eye views of the town, surrounding hills and the shimmering lake below. Paragliding offers a unique perspective of Varenna's natural beauty.

Rock Climbing at Roccia di Varenna

Challenge your climbing skills at Roccia di Varenna, a rock formation that beckons climbers with its unique features. Whether you're a beginner or an experienced climber, this natural rock face offers various routes, providing a thrilling outdoor adventure with stunning views as your reward.

Nature trails in Riserva Naturale Varenna Esino

Embark on nature trails within the Riserva Naturale Varenna Esino, a protected nature reserve that encompasses diverse ecosystems. Wander through woodlands, meadows and wetlands, encountering a variety of flora and fauna. The reserve's well-marked trails cater to hikers of all levels, making it an ideal destination for an immersive nature walk.

Varenna's outdoor activities cater to a spectrum of interests, from those seeking adrenaline-pumping adventures to those yearning for tranquil moments amid nature's embrace. As you explore the diverse landscapes and engage in outdoor pursuits, you'll find that Varenna offers a perfect blend of adventure and serenity for nature lovers and adventurers alike.

Festive echoes: Celebrating the cultural heritage of Varenna

Varenna, with its rich historical tapestry, comes alive with vibrant celebrations and time-honoured traditions that reflect the town's cultural identity. Throughout the year, locals and visitors alike gather to partake in festive rituals that have been passed down through generations. From religious processions to lively carnivals, these traditions add a touch of magic to the town, providing a glimpse into Varenna's cultural heritage. Let us embark on a journey through the traditions and festivals that define the spirit of Varenna, where each event is a celebration of community, history and the enduring bonds that tie the town together.

Festa di San Giorgio (April)

The Festa di San Giorgio honours the patron saint of Varenna. The celebration kicks off with a religious procession through the streets, featuring the statue of San Giorgio adorned with flowers. Locals participate in traditional dances and the festivities culminate in a communal feast with local delicacies, symbolizing unity and spiritual reverence.

Fiera di Santa Lucia (December)

The Fiera di Santa Lucia heralds the holiday season with a festive market. The streets are adorned with twinkling lights as vendors offer handcrafted goods, seasonal treats and festive decorations. This traditional fair captures the essence of Christmas, creating a magical atmosphere for all who attend.

Processione del Venerdì Santo (March/April)

On Good Friday, the Processione del Venerdì Santo unfolds in a solemn display of religious devotion. Locals participate in a candlelit procession through the streets, re-enacting the Stations of the Cross. The atmosphere is one of reflection and reverence, as the town comes together to observe this significant day in the Christian calendar.

Palio delle Contrade (August)

Varenna's Palio delle Contrade is a spirited competition that pits the town's neighbourhoods, or contrade, against each other in various contests and competitions. From traditional games to culinary challenges, this lively event fosters a sense of community pride and friendly rivalry among the contrade, culminating in a grand celebration.

Sagra del Pesce (July/Aaugust)

The Sagra del Pesce, held in the summer months, celebrates Varenna's connection to its lakeside location. This fish festival highlights the bounty of Lago di Varenna with an array of seafood dishes, live music and lakeside festivities. It's a time for locals and visitors to savour the flavours of the lake and revel in the town's maritime heritage.

Corsa dei Carretti (July)

Corsa dei Carretti, or the Cart Race, is a thrilling spectacle that takes place during the summer months. Participants design and race homemade carts through the town's streets, competing for speed and creativity. The event captures the town's playful spirit and provides a light-hearted yet exciting experience for participants and spectators alike.

Festa della Vendemmia (August)

As the grape harvest season approaches, Varenna hosts the Festa della Vendemmia, a celebration of the town's winemaking traditions. Locals gather to participate in traditional grape stomping, grape-picking contests and wine tastings. The festival showcases Varenna's viticultural heritage, uniting the community in a joyous celebration of the grape harvest.

Notte Bianca (July/August)

Varenna's Notte Bianca, or White Night, is an annual event that transforms the town into a nocturnal playground. The streets come alive with live music, art exhibitions and cultural performances that continue into the early hours. Notte Bianca embodies the town's dynamic cultural scene, inviting residents and visitors to embrace the magic of the night.

Carnevale di Varenna (February/March)

Carnevale di Varenna, transforms the town into a lively spectacle of colours and costumes. The streets come alive with parades, masked processions and vibrant displays of creativity. Locals and visitors don elaborate costumes, revelling in the festive atmosphere that marks the pre-Lenten season with joyous abandon.

Varenna's local traditions and festivals are a testament to the town's commitment to preserving its cultural heritage. Each celebration becomes a thread in the intricate tapestry of Varenna's history, weaving together the past and the present in a vibrant display of communal spirit and shared identity.

Bellagio's whisper: Travel tips for discovering Varenna's magic

Embarking on a journey to Varenna is not just a visit; it's an immersive exploration of history, culture and natural beauty. To make the most of your stay in this charming Italian town, we've compiled a set of travel tips that will guide you through the cobblestone streets, serene lakeshores and cultural wonders of Varenna. From understanding local customs to uncovering hidden gems, these insights ensure that your time in Varenna is filled with enriching moments and unforgettable experiences.

Blend in at the local markets

Immerse yourself in the local culture by exploring Varenna's markets. Whether it's the bustling Fiera di Santa Lucia or the traditional Sagra dell'Olio, these markets offer a chance to interact with locals, sample regional delicacies and discover handmade crafts. Blend in with the rhythm of daily life as you peruse the stalls and engage in friendly conversations with vendors and residents.

Learn a few basic Italian phrases

While many locals in Varenna may speak English, making an effort to learn a few basic Italian phrases can go a long way in fostering connections. Simple greetings, polite expressions and thank-yous are appreciated gestures that showcase your respect for the local culture. Locals often respond warmly when visitors make an effort to speak their language.

Explore beyond the Main Square

Varenna's main square is undoubtedly charming, but the town's true essence lies in its hidden corners and narrow alleys. Venture beyond the well-trodden paths to discover hidden gems, quaint cafes and unexpected surprises. The exploration of less-explored areas allows you to witness the authentic daily life of Varenna.

Take a boat ride on Lago di Varenna

Experience Varenna from a unique perspective by taking a boat ride on Lago di Varenna. The lake offers stunning views of the town, surrounded by lush hills and historic villas. Rent a boat or join a guided tour to appreciate the serene beauty of Varenna from the tranquillity of its shimmering waters.

Respect religious customs

Varenna has a rich religious heritage and it's important to respect local customs, especially during religious celebrations. If you find yourself in town during a religious procession or ceremony, observe quietly and avoid disrupting the solemnity of the occasion. Modesty and respect for sacred spaces are key aspects of cultural sensitivity.

Hike Monte Varenna for panoramic views

For breath-taking vistas of Varenna and its surrounding landscapes, embark on a hike up Monte Varenna. The well-marked trails lead you through forests and meadows, rewarding your efforts with panoramic views of the town and the picturesque Lombardy region.

Stay in a charming local accommodation

Enhance your Varenna experience by choosing accommodations that reflect the town's charm. Opt for a family-run bed and breakfast, an historic villa, or a boutique hotel to immerse yourself in the local atmosphere. Many accommodations offer personalized touches and insider recommendations for exploring Varenna.

Connect with locals through art and culture

Engage with Varenna's vibrant art scene and cultural offerings to connect with the local community. Attend art exhibitions, music performances, or theatre productions to gain insights into the town's creative spirit. Conversations with local artists and cultural enthusiasts can provide a deeper understanding of Varenna's artistic heritage.

Capture the magic of Varenna

Bring a camera or smartphone to capture the enchanting moments and picturesque landscapes of Varenna. Whether it's the reflection of historic buildings on the lake, the vibrant colours of a local market, or the intimate details of hidden gems, documenting your journey allows you to relive the magic of Varenna even after your visit.

Check local transportation options

Explore Varenna and its surroundings by considering local transportation options. Whether it's a leisurely stroll through the town, a boat ride on the lake, or a train journey to nearby destinations, utilizing different modes of transportation enhances your travel experience and provides diverse perspectives of Varenna.

Enjoy sunset views over Lago di Varenna

Witness the mesmerizing sunset over Lago di Varenna for a magical and romantic experience. Find a scenic spot along the lake's shores, sip on a glass of local wine and bask in the warm hues as the sun dips below the horizon, casting a golden glow over the town.

Varenna's charm lies in its ability to offer a rich tapestry of experiences, blending cultural heritage with natural beauty. These travel tips aim to enhance your journey, ensuring that your time in Varenna is not just a visit but a memorable and authentic exploration of this Italian gem.

Whispers of wonder: Final thoughts on the lakeside splendour in Varenna

As your journey through Varenna concludes, the echoes of its cultural symphony linger-an enduring melody that harmonizes with the gentle murmur of the Adda River. Varenna, with its historic charm and vibrant local culture, offers more than just a fleeting visit; it provides a timeless exploration into the heart of Lombardy.

The cobblestone streets, the warmth of the locals and the cultural riches showcased in every market stall become cherished memories etched in the traveller's heart. As you bid farewell to Varenna's tranquil embrace, may the essence of its cultural rhapsody accompany you-a reminder of the enchanting experiences woven into the fabric of this Lombardian gem along the Adda River.

Pitigliano: Perched splendour on the Tuscan cliff

Tuscan tranquillity: A prelude to Pitigliano's enchanted hills

Perched atop Tufa Cliffs in the picturesque landscape of Tuscany, Pitigliano emerges as a captivating embodiment of history, culture and architectural splendour. Pitigliano, a historic hilltop town in Tuscany, is located approximately 100 kilometres southeast of Florence and about 150 kilometres northwest of Rome. This ancient town, often referred to as the 'Little Jerusalem' due to its historically significant Jewish population, holds a magnetic charm for visitors seeking a journey through time. The altitude of Pitigliano is approximately 313 meters (1,027 feet) above sea level. Pitigliano's distinctive skyline, dominated by medieval towers and Renaissance structures, creates a mesmerizing silhouette against the rolling hills of the Maremma region.

As you wander through the labyrinthine alleys and cobblestone pathways of Pitigliano's historic centre, you'll discover a treasure trove of architectural wonders, including centuries-old palaces, churches, and fortifications. The town's iconic tufa stone buildings, built directly into the cliffsides, exude a sense of timeless beauty and resilience, offering a glimpse into the region's rich history and enduring craftsmanship.

Etruscan enigma: Pitigliano's time-immemorial echoes

Pitigliano, with its roots firmly embedded in antiquity, boasts a historical significance that spans millennia, making it a treasure trove for history enthusiasts. The town's origins trace back to the Etruscans, who hewed Pitigliano's dwellings and fortifications directly into the tufa cliffs for defensive purposes. This Etruscan legacy is evident in the town's unique architectural features, as well as in the ancient necropolis and caves that surround the settlement. As the Roman Empire rose to dominance, Pitigliano continued to play a strategic role, evolving into a flourishing centre under Roman rule.

Throughout the medieval period, Pitigliano witnessed the ebb and flow of power among various noble families, notably the Aldobrandeschi and Orsini, each leaving an indelible mark on the town's landscape. However, it was during the 16th century that Pitigliano gained particular historical importance with the establishment of a Jewish community seeking refuge from persecution. The Jewish quarter, known as the 'Little Jerusalem', stands today as a testament to the town's unique cultural amalgamation. Pitigliano's historical narrative unfolds through its well-preserved architecture, from the medieval fortress of the Orsini Castle to the charming alleys of the Jewish quarter, offering visitors a fascinating journey through the epochs that have shaped this captivating Tuscan gem.

Hilltop harmony: Embarking on Pitigliano's cultural odyssey

Pitigliano's local culture is a captivating blend of historical layers, architectural marvels and the influence of diverse communities that have coexisted for centuries. The town's medieval and Renaissance architecture, characterized by stone buildings that seem to emerge seamlessly from the cliffs, serves as a testament to the craftsmanship and artistic sensibilities of its inhabitants throughout the ages. Wandering through the narrow cobblestone streets, visitors encounter local artisans preserving traditional crafts, with workshops offering handmade ceramics, leather goods and intricate metalwork.

One of the most distinctive facets of Pitigliano's local culture is its Jewish heritage. The Jewish quarter, established in the 16th century, reflects a unique chapter in the town's history. Synagogues, ritual baths and kosher eateries provide a glimpse into the daily life of the Jewish community that sought refuge here. The coexistence of Catholic and Jewish cultures has contributed to a rich tapestry of local traditions and festivities. Pitigliano's calendar is marked by events that celebrate both Christian and Jewish heritage, fostering an atmosphere of inclusivity and cultural diversity. Additionally, the town's gastronomy is a reflection of the fertile Maremma region, offering locally sourced produce and wines that showcase the flavours of Tuscany. In experiencing Pitigliano's local culture, visitors embark on a journey through time and communal harmony, where the threads of history and tradition are woven into the fabric of daily life.

Rustic reverie: Exploring the enchanted charms of Pitigliano

Nestled in the heart of Tuscany, Pitigliano is a town steeped in history, where each cobblestone street and ancient edifice tells a tale of times gone by. Explore the town's architectural tapestry through its landmarks, revealing the Etruscan, medieval and Renaissance influences that have shaped Pitigliano's distinctive character. Here are the key points of interest that beckon travellers to uncover the secrets of this enchanting Italian gem.

Palazzo Orsini

Step into the lap of luxury with a visit to Palazzo Orsini, a magnificent Renaissance palace that once served as the residence of the powerful Orsini family. Admire its opulent architecture and lavish interiors, which offer a glimpse into the extravagant lifestyle of Renaissance nobility.

Synagogue and Jewish Quarter

Step back in time as you wander through Pitigliano's Jewish Quarter, also known as the 'Little Jerusalem' of Tuscany. Explore ancient synagogues, kosher butcher shops and ritual baths, which bear witness to the town's rich Jewish heritage dating back to the 16th century.

Fortezza Orsini

Perched majestically atop a tufa cliff, the Orsini Fortress commands attention with its imposing presence. Dating back to the 14th century, this medieval stronghold offers panoramic views of the surrounding countryside and houses a museum showcasing Pitigliano's military history.

Ponte delle Conte

Spanning the Lente River, the Ponte delle Conte is a picturesque stone bridge connecting the modern town to the ancient fortress. This marvel of medieval engineering provides a captivating entry into the historic heart of Pitigliano.

Aqueduct of Paduletto

Follow in the footsteps of the Medici family with a stroll along the Medici Aqueduct, a remarkable feat of Renaissance engineering. Marvel at its graceful arches and pristine waters as you traverse this historic landmark, which continues to supply Pitigliano with fresh spring water to this day.

Vie Cave

Embark on a journey through Pitigliano's ancient past with a hike along the Vie Cave, ancient Etruscan pathways carved into the tufa cliffs surrounding the town. Explore these mysterious sunken roads, which date back over 2,500 years and marvel at the ingenuity of the Etruscan civilization.

Piazza Garibaldi

Experience the vibrant heart of Pitigliano at Piazza Garibaldi. This lively square is surrounded by cafes, restaurants and historic buildings. It's the perfect place to unwind, savour local delicacies and absorb the lively atmosphere of the town.

Museo Archeologico all'Aperto Alberto Manzi

Delve into Pitigliano's rich archaeological heritage with a visit to the Museum of Archaeology and Art of the Maremma. Explore its extensive collection of artifacts, ranging from Etruscan pottery to Roman sculptures, which shed light on the town's ancient past.

Medieval Aqueduct

Discover the engineering marvels of ancient Rome with a visit to the Aqueduct of Pitigliano, an impressive structure that once supplied water to the town. Follow its stone arches as they wind their way through the countryside, a testament to the enduring legacy of Roman civilization.

Piazza della Repubblica

Immerse yourself in the vibrant atmosphere of Piazza della Repubblica, the bustling heart of Pitigliano's historic centre. Surrounded by charming cafes, shops and medieval buildings, this lively square is the perfect place to soak up the local culture and savour the flavours of Tuscany.

Pitigliano's landmarks weave a tapestry of architectural brilliance and historical richness. Each site invites travellers to step into the past, unveiling the layers of a town that has embraced the influences of diverse civilizations over centuries.

Authentic tastes: Delighting in Pitigliano's culinary traditions

Pitigliano, nestled in the picturesque landscapes of Tuscany, not only enchants with its medieval charm but also tantalizes the taste buds with a culinary tapestry deeply rooted in tradition. From savoury pasta dishes to delectable desserts, the town's gastronomic offerings are a celebration of local produce and time-honoured recipes. Join us on a culinary journey through Pitigliano's delightful flavours, where every dish tells a story of the region's rich cultural heritage.

Pecorino Toscano

Experience the pride of Tuscan cheese with Pecorino Toscano. This flavourful sheep's milk cheese is aged to perfection, resulting in a robust and slightly tangy taste. Enjoy it on its own or paired with local honey for a delightful contrast of flavours.

Zuppa di Funghi

Delight in the earthy goodness of Zuppa di Funghi, a savoury mushroom soup that captures the essence of the surrounding forests. Loaded with local mushrooms, this dish is a comforting embrace of the Tuscan countryside.

Agnello al Forno

Elevate your dining experience with Agnello al Forno, succulent roasted lamb seasoned with aromatic herbs. This dish reflects the pastoral traditions of Tuscany, where lamb is celebrated for its tenderness and depth of flavour.

Sfratto

Conclude your meal on a sweet note with Sfratto, a traditional Jewish dessert hailing from Pitigliano's Little Jerusalem. This honey and nut-filled pastry roll is a delightful treat with a history that adds layers of cultural significance to its sweet allure.

Acquacotta

Begin your gastronomic exploration with Acquacotta, a traditional Tuscan soup that translates to 'cooked water'. This hearty dish features a broth made from tomatoes, vegetables and herbs, enriched with a poached egg and crusty bread, creating a soul-warming delight.

Frittelle di Riso

Indulge your sweet tooth with Frittelle di Riso, delightful rice fritters that are deep-fried to golden perfection. Sprinkled with powdered sugar, these light and airy fritters are a beloved Tuscan dessert often enjoyed during festive occasions.

Crostata di Ricotta e Visciole

Experience the perfect marriage of creamy ricotta and tart cherries in Crostata di Ricotta e Visciole. This classic Tuscan tart is a symphony of flavours, with the sweetness of ricotta harmonizing with the vibrant notes of sour cherries.

Limoncello

Conclude your culinary journey with a sip of Limoncello, a zesty lemon liqueur that captures the essence of Pitigliano's sunny orchards. This refreshing digestif is a fitting finale to a meal, leaving a lingering taste of Tuscany on your palate.

Pappardelle al Cinghiale

Indulge in the flavours of Tuscany with Pappardelle al Cinghiale. This pasta dish showcases wide ribbons of pasta adorned with a rich ragù made from tender wild boar, creating a robust and savoury experience that reflects the region's hunting traditions.

Pitigliano's culinary delights are a testament to the region's commitment to preserving its culinary heritage. Each dish invites you to savour the authenticity and passion woven into the fabric of Tuscan gastronomy, making every bite a celebration of tradition and flavour.

Pitigliano's hidden marvels: Unveiling the unseen

As you wander through the enchanting streets of Pitigliano, you'll discover a treasure trove of hidden gems that add an extra layer of magic to this ancient Tuscan town. Beyond the well-trodden paths lie secret corners and historical whispers waiting to be unearthed. Join me on a journey to explore Pitigliano's hidden gems, where each discovery unfolds a story of mystery, history and the timeless allure of this captivating destination.

Pozzo di San Patrizio

Descend into the depths of history at Pozzo di San Patrizio, an architectural marvel designed by Antonio da Sangallo the Younger in the 16th century. This well, often referred to as St. Patrick's Well, features a double-helix staircase, allowing visitors to access water without crossing paths-an ingenious engineering feat.

Parco Orsini

Escape to Parco Orsini, a tranquil oasis nestled within the town's medieval walls. This hidden park offers shaded pathways, ancient ruins and panoramic views of the surrounding countryside. It's a serene retreat for a leisurely stroll or a quiet moment of contemplation.

Cantina Morellino

Uncover Cantina Morellino, a hidden gem for wine enthusiasts. Beneath Pitigliano's streets lie ancient wine cellars, where local winemakers produce the renowned Morellino di Scansano. Delve into a guided wine tasting, immersing yourself in the flavours and aromas of this esteemed Tuscan red wine.

Via Zuccarelli

Stroll down Via Zuccarelli, an artisan's haven tucked away from the main thoroughfares. Lined with workshops and boutiques, this charming alley reveals the craftsmanship behind local pottery, leather goods and handmade treasures. It's a hidden retreat for those seeking authentic, handcrafted souvenirs.

Fontana delle Sette Cannelle

Seek out the Fontana delle Sette Cannelle, an unassuming fountain with a fascinating history. Legend has it that the fountain was built to quench the thirst of travellers and pilgrims passing through Pitigliano. Its seven spouts represent the seven virtues.

Museum of the Etruscan Civilization

Discover the Museum of the Etruscan Civilization, a lesser-known gem that houses a remarkable collection of artifacts from Pitigliano's Etruscan past. The museum provides an immersive experience, shedding light on the daily life, art and rituals of this ancient civilization.

Chiesa di Santa Maria delle Grazie

Visit the Chiesa di Santa Maria delle Grazie, a hidden church known for its serene atmosphere and beautiful frescoes. Tucked away from the bustling streets, this sacred space invites contemplation and appreciation for the artistic heritage of Pitigliano.

Archaeological Park of the Tuff Area

Unearth the archaeological wonders of the Tuff Area, an expansive park that showcases the geological and historical significance of Pitigliano's tufa rock. Wander through ancient caves, witness the remains of Etruscan settlements and immerse yourself in the layers of Pitigliano's past.

Pitigliano's hidden gems beckon intrepid explorers to venture beyond the well-known landmarks, promising a tapestry of surprises, cultural richness and a deeper connection to the town's enigmatic charm.

Tranquil treks: Discovering outdoor delights in Pitigliano's country sides

Pitigliano, with its captivating landscapes and ancient charm, beckons outdoor enthusiasts to embark on an adventure beyond its historical streets. The town, nestled amidst the picturesque hills of Tuscany, offers a myriad of outdoor activities that allow visitors to connect with nature, soak in panoramic views and revel in the region's natural beauty. Let us explore Pitigliano's outdoor wonders-each activity a gateway to a world where the allure of the outdoors harmonizes with the town's rich history.

Cycling the Tuscan hills

Saddle up for a cycling adventure through the undulating hills surrounding Pitigliano. The charming countryside offers a network of scenic routes, winding through vineyards, olive groves and historic hamlets. Whether you're a leisurely cyclist or a thrill-seeker, Pitigliano's terrain caters to all biking enthusiasts.

Hot air balloon experience

Ascend to the skies with a hot air balloon ride that provides a breath-taking perspective of Pitigliano's medieval beauty and the rolling Tuscan landscape. As you soar above the tufa cliffs and lush valleys, revel in the tranquillity and grandeur of this timeless destination.

Kayaking the Fiora river

Paddle through the gentle currents of the Fiora River, offering a unique perspective of Pitigliano's natural surroundings. The river meanders through verdant landscapes, providing kayakers with a serene and immersive experience amidst nature's splendour.

Via Clodia: Historical walking trail

Embark on the Via Clodia, a historical walking trail that traces the ancient Roman road connecting Pitigliano to Rome. This scenic route takes you through olive groves, vineyards and charming hamlets, offering glimpses of both natural and historical wonders.

Birdwatching in Sovana's nature reserve

Sovana, a short distance from Pitigliano, is home to a nature reserve that beckons birdwatchers. Explore the diverse ecosystems and catch glimpses of migratory birds, creating a peaceful and meditative experience amidst nature's symphony.

Rock climbing in Tufa cliffs

Challenge your adventurous spirit with rock climbing in Pitigliano's tufa cliffs. The unique geological formations provide an exhilarating ascent for climbers, rewarding them with unparalleled views of the town and surrounding landscapes.

Stargazing in the Tuscan night sky

As the sun sets over Pitigliano, witness the magic of the Tuscan night sky. Far from city lights, the town offers an ideal setting for stargazing. Whether with a guided astronomy tour or a peaceful evening under the stars, Pitigliano invites you to marvel at the celestial wonders above.

Pitigliano's outdoor activities promise an immersive and diverse experience for nature enthusiasts, inviting them to explore the region's beauty while forging a deeper connection with its history and landscapes.

Radiant revels: Experiencing the brilliance of Pitigliano's traditions

Pitigliano, a town steeped in history and charm, comes alive with a vibrant tapestry of local traditions and festivals that reflect the heart and soul of its community. These events, rooted in centuries-old customs and cultural expressions, offer a unique window into the town's identity. Delve into Pitigliano's lively calendar of festivities, where time-honoured rituals, music and joyous gatherings bring the community together in a celebration of their rich heritage.

Festa di San Giuseppe (March)

Experience the Festa di San Giuseppe, a celebration dedicated to Saint Joseph, the patron saint of the town. This religious festivity combines solemn processions with joyful gatherings, where locals come together to honour their saint with traditional rituals, music and a vibrant display of flowers.

Sagra delle Cantine (May)

Indulge in the flavours of Pitigliano at the Sagra delle Cantine, a festival celebrating local wines and culinary delights. The town's historic cellars open their doors, inviting visitors to savour regional wines, traditional dishes and the warm hospitality that defines Pitigliano's culinary scene.

Festival delle Bandiere (June)

Marvel at the spectacle of the festival delle Bandiere, a colourful event that showcases the town's ancient flag-waving traditions. Performers dressed in historical attire parade through the streets, skilfully twirling flags to the beat of traditional music, creating a mesmerizing display of cultural pride.

Palio delle Contrade (July)

Witness the fervour of the Palio delle Contrade, an annual horse race that encapsulates the spirit of competition and camaraderie. Held in the historic centre, this event sees the town's neighbourhoods, or contrade, vie for victory, creating a lively atmosphere of cheers and festivities that captivate both locals and visitors.

Notte Bianca (August)

Dive into the lively atmosphere of Notte Bianca, an all-night celebration that animates the town with music, performances and a joyful spirit. From street artists to live music, this event showcases Pitigliano's creative energy and community cohesion under the moonlit sky.

Settembre DiVino (September)

Celebrate the rich viticultural heritage of Pitigliano at Settembre DiVino, a wine festival that invites enthusiasts to taste the region's finest vintages. With wine tastings, cellar tours and cultural events, this festival pays homage to the art of winemaking that has flourished in the town for generations.

Festa di Santa Maria (September)

Join in the devotion of the Festa di Santa Maria, a religious celebration dedicated to the Assumption of the Virgin Mary. This solemn event combines religious processions with moments of prayer, creating a sense of unity and spiritual reflection within the community.

Mercato delle Vecchie Cose (October)

Step back in time at the Mercato delle Vecchie Cose, a market that brings antique treasures to life. Held in the historic centre, this event allows visitors to explore a myriad of vintage items, from clothing to trinkets, offering a glimpse into Pitigliano's historical material culture.

Pitigliano's local traditions and festivals weave a colourful tapestry that enhances the town's cultural identity. From religious processions to lively celebrations, each event contributes to the vibrant and diverse heritage that defines Pitigliano as a town of enduring traditions and joyful festivities.

Tuscan treasures: Navigating Pitigliano's enchanting alleys with savvy

Nestled atop volcanic cliffs in the heart of Tuscany, Pitigliano beckons travellers with its medieval charm and Etruscan heritage. To make the most of your visit to this captivating town, here are travel tips that unveil the secrets of Pitigliano. From savouring local delicacies to exploring ancient alleyways, let these insights guide you through the timeless beauty of Pitigliano.

Plan your visit in advance

Pitigliano is a popular tourist destination, especially during the summer months. To make the most of your trip and avoid crowds, consider visiting during the shoulder seasons of spring or fall. Additionally, book accommodations and tours in advance, especially if you plan to visit during peak times.

Wear comfortable footwear

Pitigliano's historic centre is characterized by narrow cobblestone streets and steep staircases, so wearing comfortable walking shoes is essential for exploring the town comfortably. Be prepared for some uphill walking and uneven surfaces, especially if you plan to visit the town's medieval fortress.

Respect local customs and traditions

Pitigliano is a town rich in history and cultural heritage and it's important to respect local customs and traditions during your visit. Dress modestly when visiting religious sites such as churches and cathedrals and observe any cultural practices or etiquette guidelines.

Stay hydrated and protect yourself from the sun

Pitigliano can get quite hot during the summer months, so it's important to stay hydrated and protect yourself from the sun. Carry a reusable water bottle with you and drink plenty of fluids throughout the day. Additionally, wear sunscreen, a hat and sunglasses to protect your skin and eyes from the sun's harmful rays.

Explore beyond the historic centre

While Pitigliano's historic centre is undoubtedly charming, don't miss the opportunity to explore the surrounding countryside and nearby attractions. Rent a car or join a guided tour to visit nearby towns, wineries and natural landmarks such as the Maremma Regional Park and Lake Bolsena.

Learn basic Italian phrases

While many locals in Pitigliano speak English, learning a few basic Italian phrases can enhance your experience and help you connect with locals. Practice common greetings, expressions of gratitude and basic conversational phrases to make interactions with locals more enjoyable.

Take advantage of guided tours

Consider joining a guided tour or hiring a local guide to learn more about Pitigliano's history, architecture and cultural significance. Guided tours offer valuable insights and can help you navigate the town's narrow streets and hidden gems with ease.

Respect the environment

Help preserve Pitigliano's natural beauty and pristine environment by practicing responsible tourism. Dispose of waste properly, recycle when possible and refrain from littering in public spaces. Leave natural areas as you found them to ensure they remain accessible for future generations to enjoy.

Stay flexible and open-minded

Lastly, stay flexible and open-minded during your visit to Pitigliano. Embrace unexpected encounters, serendipitous discoveries and the slower pace of life in this charming Tuscan town. Allow yourself to be immersed in the beauty and tranquillity of Pitigliano and you're sure to have a memorable experience.

Pitigliano's timeless allure is an invitation to step back in time and immerse yourself in Tuscany's rich cultural tapestry. These travel tips provide a roadmap to unlock the town's secrets, ensuring your journey through Pitigliano is a memorable exploration of history, flavours and natural beauty.

Whispers of wonder: Concluding the chapter with captivating reflections in Pitigliano

In these closing reflections, Pitigliano stands not only as a repository of history but as a living testament to the coexistence of diverse cultures. The Jewish quarter, with its synagogues and ritual baths, serves as a poignant reminder of the town's role as a haven for those seeking refuge.

As the sun sets over the Tuscan landscape, casting its warm glow on Pitigliano's medieval fortress and charming streets, one can't help but be captivated by the enduring spirit of this ancient town. In the spirit of Pitigliano's cultural mosaic, may the memories of this journey linger as a timeless treasure, resonating with the echoes of centuries past and the vibrant harmony of a town that continues to enchant all who walk its storied streets.

Polignano: Coastal elegance, Mediterranean magic

Polignano panorama: Enchanting coastal escapes

Nestled along the rugged Adriatic coastline of southern Italy, Polignano a Mare stands as a picturesque gem embodying the timeless allure of coastal living. With its dramatic cliffs, crystal-clear waters, and labyrinthine streets steeped in history, this charming town beckons travellers to immerse themselves in its rich tapestry of culture and natural beauty. Perched atop sheer limestone cliffs that overlook the azure Adriatic Sea, Polignano captivates visitors with its breath-taking vistas and dramatic panoramas. Over the centuries, Polignano has been shaped by various civilizations, from the Greeks and Romans to the Normans and Byzantines, each leaving their indelible mark on its architecture, traditions, and way of life.

Today, Polignano enchants visitors with its unique blend of history, culture, and coastal charm. Wander through its narrow cobblestone streets adorned with whitewashed buildings, you will discover hidden piazzas, quaint cafes, and artisanal shops showcasing local crafts. The town's vibrant cultural scene comes to life during festivals and events celebrating its maritime heritage, music, and gastronomy. Whether you're indulging in fresh seafood delicacies at seaside trattorias, taking a dip in the crystalline waters of its hidden coves, or simply savouring a sunset cocktail overlooking the Adriatic, Polignano offers a quintessential Italian experience that lingers in the hearts and memories of all who visit.

Legacies of the past: Polignano's historic impact

Polignano, with its ancient origins dating back to prehistoric times, bears witness to a remarkable historical journey that has shaped its identity and character. Situated strategically along the Adriatic coast of Italy, the town has been inhabited by various civilizations throughout the ages, each leaving a distinct imprint on its landscape and heritage. Traces of ancient settlements, including Neolithic caves and Roman ruins, speak volumes about Polignano's enduring legacy as a site of human habitation for millennia.

During the medieval period, Polignano flourished under Norman rule, becoming a thriving centre of commerce and culture in the region. The town's location made it a coveted prize for competing powers, resulting in centuries of conquests and conflicts that have left their mark on its architecture and fortifications. Today, visitors can explore the remnants of Polignano's medieval past, from its ancient city walls and watchtowers to its historic churches and palazzos, each bearing testament to the town's storied history. Polignano's historical significance is further underscored by its role as a crossroads of civilizations, where East meets West and ancient traditions blend seamlessly with modern life. From its Greek and Roman roots to its Byzantine, Norman, and Aragonese influences, the town's cultural tapestry is a testament to the resilience and adaptability of its people throughout the ages.

Shores of heritage: Exploring Polignano's cultural mosaic

Imbued with a rich tapestry of traditions and a deep-rooted connection to its maritime heritage, Polignano's local culture reflects the soul of its coastal community. At the heart of Polignano's cultural identity lies a reverence for the sea, which has shaped the lives and livelihoods of its inhabitants for centuries. Fishing has long been a central aspect of local life, and the town's bustling fish market offers a glimpse into this age-old tradition, where fishermen bring in their daily catch and locals gather to haggle over the freshest seafood.

The town has inspired generations of artists, poets, and musicians with its breath-taking beauty and evocative atmosphere. Throughout the year, Polignano plays host to a variety of cultural events and festivals celebrating its artistic heritage, from classical music concerts to contemporary art exhibitions held in historic venues and outdoor spaces.

In addition to its artistic endeavours, Polignano's local culture is deeply intertwined with its culinary traditions, which showcase the region's bounty of fresh, seasonal ingredients. Traditional dishes such as orecchiette pasta with seafood, grilled octopus, and creamy burrata cheese reflect the flavours of the Adriatic coast, while local wines such as Primitivo and Negroamaro offer a taste of Puglia's viticultural heritage. Whether partaking in a lively street festival, savouring a home-cooked meal with locals, or exploring the town's artisanal workshops and boutiques, visitors to Polignano are welcomed into a vibrant community that takes pride in its cultural heritage and embraces the timeless rhythms of coastal living.

Cliffside wonders: Revealing Polignano's captivating landmarks

Polignano a Mare emerges as a picturesque town steeped in history and adorned with breath-taking natural beauty. With its ancient origins, Polignano boasts a rich tapestry of cultural heritage and architectural wonders that captivate visitors from around the world. From dramatic sea caves to historic landmarks and charming cobblestone streets, each corner of Polignano tells a story of its past and invites travellers to immerse themselves in its timeless charm.

Grotta Palazzese

The Grotta Palazzese is an awe-inspiring natural cave that has been transformed into a world-renowned restaurant. Carved out of limestone by the relentless force of the Adriatic Sea, the cave boasts a stunning natural setting with panoramic views of the azure waters below. Guests can dine on gourmet cuisine while seated on the cave's terrace, surrounded by the enchanting beauty of the sea and the echoing sound of waves.

Ponte Lama Monachile

The Ponte Lama Monachile is a historic bridge that spans the gorge of Lama Monachile, connecting the historic centre of Polignano with the seafront promenade. Dating back to the 16th century, the bridge offers breath-taking views of the coastline and the crystal-clear waters of the Adriatic Sea. Visitors can stroll across the bridge, taking in the scenic vistas and capturing memorable photos of Polignano's iconic landscape.

Statue of Domenico Modugno

Dominating Piazza Domenico Modugno is a bronze statue honouring the famed Italian singer and songwriter. Domenico Modugno, a native of Polignano, is best known for his iconic song "Volare," which has become synonymous with the town and its cultural identity. The statue, unveiled in 2011, captures Modugno in mid-performance, exuding his passion and charisma. Set against the backdrop of Polignano's historic centre, the statue serves as a tribute to Modugno's enduring legacy and his contribution to Italian music and culture.

Lama Monachile Beach

Lama Monachile Beach, also known as Cala Porto, is a small but striking pebble beach nestled between towering cliffs in the heart of Polignano's historic centre. Accessible via a narrow staircase, the beach offers a secluded escape from the bustling streets of the town. Visitors can relax on the pebbles, soak up the sun, and take a refreshing swim in the crystal-clear waters of the Adriatic.

San Vito Martire Church

San Vito Martire Church, nestled amidst the historic centre of Polignano, is a captivating example of Romanesque architecture dating back to the 12th century. Its façade, adorned with intricate stone carvings, serves as a testament to the craftsmanship of the era. Inside, visitors are greeted by a serene atmosphere and can admire an array of religious artworks, including frescoes depicting scenes from the life of San Vito. The church's tranquil ambiance and architectural beauty make it a must-visit destination.

Polignano Tower

Standing tall as a sentinel over the town, Polignano Tower offers a glimpse into the town's medieval past. Constructed in the 13th century by the Normans, this imposing watchtower served as a defensive stronghold against invaders. Today, visitors can ascend its ancient stone staircase to reach the top, where panoramic views of Polignano's historic centre and coastline await. From this vantage point, one can marvel at the beauty of the Adriatic Sea while contemplating the tower's role in safeguarding the town throughout the centuries.

Piazza Aldo Moro

Piazza Aldo Moro serves as the vibrant heart of Polignano a Mare, pulsating with life and energy. Flanked by charming buildings and bustling cafes, this bustling square is a favourite gathering spot for locals and tourists alike. At its centre stands a statue commemorating Aldo Moro, a prominent figure in Italian politics. Visitors can immerse themselves in the lively atmosphere of the piazza, enjoying a leisurely coffee or gelato while soaking in the sights and sounds of Polignano's vibrant community.

Bastione San Giorgio

Perched atop a rocky promontory, Bastione San Giorgio offers panoramic views of the Adriatic Sea and Polignano's stunning coastline. Built in the 16th century as a defensive fortress, this historic landmark provides insight into the town's maritime history and strategic importance. Visitors can explore the fortress's ancient ramparts and fortified walls, which once served as a formidable barrier against enemy attacks.

Polignano a Mare Historic Centre

The historic centre of Polignano a Mare is a charming labyrinth of narrow cobblestone streets, ancient churches, and picturesque squares. Steeped in history, this district invites visitors to explore its rich cultural heritage and architectural wonders. Highlights include the Church of San Vito Martire, the Polignano Tower, and the Palazzo Marchesale. Visitors can wander through the maze-like streets, admiring the medieval architecture and soaking up the atmosphere of this timeless Italian town.

Polignano a Mare stands as a treasure trove of history, culture, and natural beauty along the sun-kissed shores of the Adriatic. With its rich tapestry of cultural heritage and breath-taking landscapes, Polignano a Mare captivates the hearts and imaginations of all who venture to its shores, leaving an indelible mark on those who are fortunate enough to experience its wonders.

Flavours of the Adriatic: Temptations from Polignano's culinary coastline

The charming town of Polignano a Mare beckons travellers with its breath-taking views of the Adriatic Sea and its rich culinary heritage. Known for its fresh seafood, fragrant olive oil, and rustic farm-to-table cuisine, Polignano offers a gastronomic journey that celebrates the flavours of the Mediterranean. From quaint trattorias tucked away in narrow alleyways to elegant waterfront restaurants overlooking the azure waters, every dining experience in Polignano promises to tantalize the taste buds and leave a lasting impression.

Friselle with Burrata and Cherry Tomatoes

A beloved Puglian specialty, friselle are crunchy twice-baked bread rounds that are soaked in water and topped with creamy burrata cheese, ripe cherry tomatoes, fresh basil, and a drizzle of extra virgin olive oil. This simple yet flavourful dish perfectly captures the essence of Puglian cuisine, with its emphasis on quality ingredients and bold flavours.

Seafood Risotto

With its prime location along the Adriatic coast, it's no surprise that seafood features prominently in Polignano's cuisine. One of the standout dishes is seafood risotto, made with locally caught fish and shellfish, fragrant saffron, and Arborio rice cooked to creamy perfection. Served with a glass of crisp Puglian white wine, this dish is a true celebration of the sea.

Ricci di Mare

Polignano's coastal location offers access to some of the freshest seafood, including the prized ricci di mare, or sea urchins. Served raw or incorporated into pasta dishes, these briny delicacies boast a rich and complex flavour that captures the essence of the sea.

Orecchiette with Cime di Rapa

Orecchiette, or "little ears," are a type of pasta that is synonymous with Puglian cuisine. Served with cime di rapa, or turnip greens, and seasoned with garlic, chili flakes, and anchovies, this hearty and satisfying dish is a staple of Polignano's culinary scene. The bitterness of the green pairs perfectly with the richness of the pasta, creating a dish that is both comforting and delicious.

Panzerotti

Similar to a calzone or fried turnover, panzerotti are savoury pastries filled with ingredients like tomato sauce, mozzarella, and often a variety of meats or vegetables. In Polignano, these delectable treats are typically deep-fried to crispy perfection, creating a satisfying contrast of textures and flavours.

Polpette di Melanzane

A vegetarian delight, polpette di melanzane are eggplant-based meatballs seasoned with herbs and spices, then fried until golden brown. Served with a tangy tomato sauce and a sprinkle of grated cheese, these savoury morsels are a beloved appetizer or side dish in Polignano's culinary repertoire.

Taralli

These small, savoury biscuits are a beloved snack throughout Puglia, and Polignano is no exception. Made with flour, olive oil, and white wine, taralli are often flavoured with fennel seeds or black pepper, resulting in a deliciously crunchy and addictive treat that pairs perfectly with a glass of wine or aperitivo.

Burrata e Pomodori

A simple yet sublime dish, burrata e pomodori showcases the creamy goodness of burrata cheese paired with ripe, juicy tomatoes, fresh basil, and a drizzle of extra virgin olive oil. This classic combination highlights the quality of Puglia's dairy products and seasonal produce, making it a must-try for cheese lovers and food enthusiasts alike.

Pasticiotto

No visit to Polignano would be complete without indulging in a pasticiotto, a traditional Puglian pastry filled with sweet custard cream. Crisp and flaky on the outside and creamy and decadent on the inside, pasticiotto is the perfect way to end a meal in Polignano or enjoy as a sweet treat with a morning espresso.

Exploring the culinary delights of Polignano is not just a journey for the taste buds, but a window into the vibrant culture and traditions of Puglia. Every bite in Polignano is a celebration of life, love, and the joy of sharing good food with good company. So, come hungry, leave satisfied, and carry with your memories of flavours that will linger long after your visit to this enchanting corner of Italy. Buon appetito!

Secrets of the seaside: Discovering Polignano's coastal treasures

Polignano is renowned for its stunning landscapes and vibrant culture. However, beyond the well-trodden paths lie hidden gems waiting to be discovered by intrepid travellers. These hidden gems offer a glimpse into the authentic heart of Polignano, where timeless traditions and natural wonders converge to create unforgettable experiences.

Borgo Antico

Step back in time as you wander through the winding alleys of Borgo Antico, Polignano's historic quarter. This charming neighbourhood is dotted with ancient buildings, picturesque squares, and hidden courtyards, offering a glimpse into the town's rich cultural heritage. Discover quaint cafes, artisan shops, and centuries-old churches tucked away in this hidden gem of Polignano.

Cala Fetente

Secluded Cove Tucked away along the coastline, Cala Fetente is a hidden gem known for its pristine waters and secluded atmosphere. Accessible only by boat or a rugged hiking trail, this tranquil cove offers a peaceful retreat for those seeking solitude amidst nature's beauty.

Il Pozzo dei Desideri

The Wishing Well Located in the heart of Polignano's historic centre, Il Pozzo dei Desideri (The Wishing Well) is a charming spot steeped in legend. According to local folklore, those who toss a coin into the well and make a wish are said to have their desires granted. Visitors can partake in this age-old tradition while admiring the well's intricate design and surrounding cobblestone streets.

Porto di San Vito

A secluded harbour escape from the hustle and bustle of the town centre, explore the tranquil harbour of Porto di San Vito. Tucked away from the main tourist areas, this secluded spot offers breath-taking views of the Adriatic Sea and the rugged coastline. Visitors can watch local fishermen at work, stroll along the scenic promenade, or simply unwind and enjoy the peaceful ambiance of this hidden gem.

Porta Vecchia

Ancient City Gate Step back in time as you pass through Porta Vecchia, Polignano's ancient city gate. Dating back to the medieval era, this historic landmark once served as the main entrance to the town. Today, it stands as a testament to Polignano's rich heritage and offers a glimpse into its storied past.

Piazza Vittorio Emanuele II

Hidden Square Tucked away from the main thoroughfares, Piazza Vittorio Emanuele II is a hidden square brimming with local charm. Lined with quaint cafes, artisan shops, and historic buildings, this hidden gem offers a tranquil escape from the bustling streets. Visitors can relax in the shade of centuries-old trees, sip espresso at a sidewalk cafe, or simply soak in the ambiance of this hidden oasis.

Valle d'Itria

Picturesque Countryside Venture beyond the town centre and explore the picturesque countryside of Valle d'Itria, a hidden gem known for its rolling hills, olive groves, and charming trulli houses. Take a leisurely drive through the scenic landscapes, stopping to admire the quaint villages and ancient olive trees that dot the countryside. Whether by car, bike, or on foot, exploring Valle d'Itria promises unforgettable views and a peaceful escape from the crowds.

Torre Incina

Perched atop a rocky outcrop overlooking the sea, Torre Incina is a centuries-old watchtower that once served as a lookout point for defending against pirate raids. Today, it remains a hidden gem offering panoramic views of the coastline and surrounding countryside. Visitors can climb to the top for breath-taking vistas or simply admire the tower's imposing presence from below.

These hidden gems of Polignano beckon travellers to explore beyond the beaten path and discover the town's authentic charm and natural beauty. Whether seeking secluded coves, historic landmarks, or tranquil squares, Polignano offers a wealth of hidden treasures waiting to be uncovered.

Coastal thrills: Unleashing outdoor adventures in Polignano

With its rugged cliffs, crystal-clear waters, and charming old town perched atop limestone cliffs, Polignano beckons outdoor enthusiasts to explore its natural wonders and indulge in a myriad of adventurous activities. From exhilarating cliff diving and coastal hiking to tranquil kayaking and beach relaxation, Polignano offers a diverse range of outdoor experiences that promise unforgettable moments amidst breath-taking scenery.

Cliff diving

Experience the adrenaline rush as you leap from Polignano's towering cliffs into the azure waters below, surrounded by breath-taking coastal views and the thrill of adventure.

Boat tours

Embark on a captivating boat tour along the rugged coastline of Polignano, where you'll discover hidden sea caves, pristine beaches, and dramatic limestone cliffs, all while enjoying the gentle sway of the Adriatic waves.

Kayaking

Glide through the crystal-clear waters of Polignano's coastline on a thrilling kayaking adventure, exploring hidden coves, secluded beaches, and majestic sea caves while marvelling at the stunning natural beauty of the Adriatic Sea.

Paragliding

Soar high above Polignano's coastal cliffs on an exhilarating paragliding flight, where you'll enjoy panoramic views of the town, turquoise waters, and rugged landscapes below, making for an unforgettable aerial experience.

Snorkelling

Dive into the vibrant underwater world of Polignano's clear blue waters, where colourful marine life, thriving coral reefs, and ancient shipwrecks await, providing an immersive snorkelling experience like no other.

Rock climbing

Challenge yourself on Polignano's limestone cliffs as you embark on an exciting rock-climbing adventure, navigating vertical walls and overhangs while enjoying panoramic views of the Adriatic coastline.

Sailing

Set sail on a relaxing sailing excursion along Polignano's stunning coastline, where you'll feel the wind in your hair and the sun on your face as you glide across the azure waters of the Adriatic Sea, exploring hidden coves and picturesque bays along the way.

Stand-up Paddleboarding (SUP)

Explore Polignano's coastal beauty from a unique perspective as you paddle along calm waters on a stand-up paddleboard, enjoying serene moments and breath-taking views of the rugged coastline and scenic landscapes.

Beach volleyball

Gather friends and family for a fun-filled game of beach volleyball on Polignano's sandy shores, where you'll enjoy friendly competition, warm sunshine, and refreshing sea breezes against the backdrop of the stunning Adriatic coastline.

As you bid farewell to Polignano, take with you the memories of its stunning coastline, warm hospitality, and exhilarating outdoor adventures. Whether you immersed yourself in the thrill of cliff diving, discovered hidden gems along the coast, or simply relaxed on its pristine beaches, Polignano leaves an indelible mark on your soul, reminding you of the beauty and serenity found in nature's embrace.

Spectacular seaside: Unravelling Polignano's festive heritage

Polignano a Mare is a town steeped in history, culture, and a vibrant tapestry of local traditions and festivals. From ancient rituals rooted in folklore to modern celebrations that pay homage to the town's rich heritage, Polignano's calendar is brimming with events that capture the essence of its spirited community. Join us as we delve into the captivating traditions and festivals that shape the rhythm of life in this enchanting Italian town, each one a testament to Polignano's enduring charm and deep-seated pride.

La Sagra del Carciofo (April)

La Sagra del Carciofo, or Artichoke Festival, is an annual culinary event held in Polignano to celebrate the region's prized artichokes. Taking place in the spring, the festival showcases a variety of dishes made with locally grown artichokes, including fried artichoke hearts, stuffed artichokes, and artichoke risotto. Visitors can sample these delicious creations at food stalls set up throughout the town, while live music and entertainment add to the festive atmosphere.

La Fiera di Santa Lucia (December)

La Fiera di Santa Lucia, or the Fair of Saint Lucia, is a traditional market held in Polignano on December 13th. The streets of Polignano are filled with vendors selling a variety of goods, including toys, decorations, and holiday treats. Families come together to enjoy the festive atmosphere, with children eagerly awaiting the arrival of Babbo Natale (Santa Claus) and the chance to see the illuminated decorations adorning the town.

La Fiera di San Biagio (February)

La Fiera di San Biagio, or the Fair of Saint Blaise, is an annual event held in Polignano on February 3rd. The fair honours Saint Blaise, the patron saint of Polignano, and features a bustling market selling a variety of goods, including local crafts, clothing, and food items. Visitors can also enjoy live music performances, traditional dances, and carnival games throughout the day. Festa di San Vito.

La Festa della Taranta (August)

La Festa della Taranta is a vibrant celebration of traditional music and dance that takes place in Polignano. Inspired by the ancient tarantella dance, which is believed to cure the bite of the tarantula spider, this festival features performances by local musicians and dancers. The streets of Polignano come alive with the sounds of tambourines, accordions, and guitars, as revelers join in the spirited dances.

Festa di San Vito (June)

The Festa di San Vito is a cherished tradition in Polignano that honours the town's patron saint, Saint Vitus. The festivities commence with a solemn religious procession through the historic streets, adorned with colourful banners and statues of the saint. Locals and visitors alike gather to witness the spectacle, offering prayers and tributes to Saint Vito. Following the procession, the town bursts into joyful celebration, with lively music, traditional dances, and a feast of local delicacies served in the piazzas.

La Fiera di San Giuseppe (March)

La Fiera di San Giuseppe, or the Feast of Saint Joseph, is a vibrant fair held annually in Polignano to commemorate the town's patron saint. The festivities centre around Piazza Vittorio Emanuele II, where a bustling market springs to life with stalls selling a variety of goods, from local crafts to artisanal foods. Throughout the day, there are performances of folk music and dance, adding to the lively atmosphere.

La Festa della Madonna della Madia (September)

Tise festival commemorates the arrival of the Madonna della Madia, a revered icon of the Virgin Mary, to the town in the 12th century. The highlight of the festivities is a solemn procession that winds its way through the streets of Polignano, with the statue of the Madonna carried aloft by devotees. Residents adorn their balconies with colourful banners and floral displays, paying homage to the Madonna. The day culminates in a mass at the Chiesa Matrice, followed by fireworks and traditional music performances.

Journey journals: Mapping your adventure in Polignano

With its enchanting old town, stunning beaches, and rich history, Polignano offers visitors a quintessential Italian experience infused with seaside charm. Whether you're seeking thrilling outdoor adventures, indulging in delectable local cuisine, or simply soaking up the sun on pristine beaches, this guide will help you make the most of your visit to this hidden gem in Puglia.

Getting there

Polignano is conveniently located in the southern Italian region of Puglia, approximately 33 kilometres south of Bari. The nearest airport is Bari Karol Wojtyła Airport (BRI), which offers domestic and international flights. From Bari, you can reach Polignano by train, bus, or car, with the journey taking about 30-40 minutes.

Best time to visit

The best time to visit Polignano is during the spring and autumn months (April to June and September to October) when the weather is mild, and tourist crowds are thinner. Summer (July to August) is peak tourist season, with warm temperatures and lively atmosphere, but beaches and attractions can be crowded.

Exploring the Old Town

Take a leisurely stroll through Polignano's charming old town, characterized by narrow cobblestone streets, whitewashed buildings adorned with colourful flowers, and stunning sea views. Don't miss the iconic Lama Monachile beach, a small pebble cove nestled between towering cliffs, often referred to as the "Pearl of the Adriatic."

Beach etiquette

When visiting Polignano's beautiful beaches, remember to respect the environment and fellow beachgoers. Dispose of litter properly, refrain from playing loud music, and avoid overcrowded areas. Additionally, some beaches may have rocky terrain, so wearing appropriate footwear is recommended.

Engaging with locals

Embrace the warm hospitality of the locals by interacting with shop owners, restaurant staff, and residents. Polignano's residents are known for their friendliness and willingness to share insights about their town, including hidden gems, cultural traditions, and local festivals.

Diving and snorkelling

Explore the crystal-clear waters surrounding Polignano through diving and snorkelling excursions. Discover vibrant marine life, underwater caves, and fascinating rock formations along the coast. Several diving centres in Polignano offer guided dives for both beginners and experienced divers.

Sunset boat tours

Experience the magic of Polignano's coastline aboard a sunset boat tour. Cruise along the Adriatic Sea as the sun dips below the horizon, casting a golden glow over the cliffs and sea caves. Many tour operators offer sunset cruises with opportunities for swimming and snorkelling in secluded coves.

Coastal hiking trails

Lace up your hiking boots and explore Polignano's scenic coastal trails, offering panoramic views of the Adriatic Sea and surrounding countryside. The Sentiero di Ronda, a coastal path that winds along the cliffs, provides an exhilarating hiking experience with breath-taking vistas at every turn.

Photography spots

Capture the beauty of Polignano's landscapes and architecture at iconic photography spots around town. From panoramic viewpoints overlooking the sea to charming alleyways adorned with colourful laundry hanging out to dry, Polignano offers endless opportunities for stunning photography.

Day trips to nearby attractions

Take advantage of Polignano's central location in Puglia to embark on day trips to nearby attractions. Explore the UNESCO-listed trulli of Alberobello, the baroque city of Lecce, or the historic town of Matera, known for its ancient cave dwellings and dramatic scenery.

Farewell to Polignano: Navigating the end of our seaside odyssey

As the sun sets over the horizon, casting a golden glow over the limestone cliffs and turquoise waters, you may find yourself reluctant to bid farewell to this coastal paradise. The sense of tranquillity and serenity that permeates the air is a reminder of the simple pleasures found in slowing down and savouring life's moments. Whether you've been drawn to Polignano for its natural beauty, rich history, or warm hospitality, one thing is certain – the memories made here will stay with you long after you've departed.

Ravello: Riviera beauty and timeless elegance

Amalfi ascent: A prelude to Ravello's enchanted clifftops

Nestled high above the glittering Tyrrhenian Sea, Ravello stands as a crowning jewel located approximately 6 kilometres inland from the Amalfi Coast, captivating visitors with its breath-taking views, cultural richness and timeless allure. This cliffside town, perched between mountains and sea, unfolds a panorama of natural beauty and architectural splendour that has been celebrated for centuries. Situated at an altitude of approximately 350 meters above sea level, Ravello offers a peaceful retreat from the crowds of the coast, where visitors can immerse themselves in the beauty of their surroundings and soak in the serenity of this enchanting village. Renowned for its lush gardens, historic villas and a backdrop that inspired countless artists, Ravello beckons travellers seeking an escape into the embrace of Italian romance and sophistication.

As one meanders through Ravello's enchanting streets, it becomes evident that this town is more than just a destination; it's an invitation to immerse oneself in a harmonious blend of history and landscape. The echoes of ancient history resonate through the medieval architecture and the town's rich cultural heritage is reflected in its churches, palaces and vibrant piazzas. Ravello, with its timeless charm and commanding views of the Amalfi Coast, offers a haven for those seeking to explore the interplay between nature's grandeur and human ingenuity on the sun-drenched cliffs of southern Italy.

Historic heights: Ravello's tale of timeless antiquity

Ravello, with its roots reaching back to ancient times, holds a profound historical significance that unfolds through the pages of the Amalfi Coast's narrative. Originally established by Roman aristocrats seeking refuge from the invading barbarians in the 5th century, Ravello's strategic location on the cliffs allowed it to flourish as a defensive stronghold. The town played a crucial role during the medieval era as part of the Maritime Republic of Amalfi, contributing to regional maritime trade and cultural exchange. However, it was during the 11th century that Ravello truly rose to prominence as a cultural and intellectual hub, attracting renowned scholars, artists and musicians to its vibrant community.

The architectural treasures that grace Ravello's landscape today bear witness to its storied past. Notable landmarks include the medieval Cathedral of Santa Maria Assunta, adorned with intricate bronze doors and ancient frescoes and the elegant Villa Rufolo, an estate dating back to the 13th century that became a gathering place for artists and intellectuals. The town's historical tapestry is interwoven with the Renaissance and Baroque influences and its churches and palazzi showcase the wealth and artistic patronage that defined Ravello during its golden age. Ravello's enduring legacy as a cultural haven contributes to the town's timeless charm, offering modern-day visitors a glimpse into the layers of history that have shaped this cliffside retreat.

Clifftop charisma: Discovering Ravello's cultural enchantment

Ravello's local culture is a captivating fusion of artistic expression, musical heritage and a profound appreciation for the scenic beauty that surrounds this idyllic town. The town's rich cultural tapestry is deeply woven into its annual events, most notably the Ravello Festival, which has been enchanting audiences since 1953. Held in iconic venues like the Villa Rufolo and Villa Cimbrone, this internationally acclaimed festival celebrates classical music, dance and visual arts, attracting artists and enthusiasts from around the world to revel in the magic of Ravello's cultural ambiance.

The warmth of the local hospitality is evident in the welcoming trattorias and family-run establishments, where time-honoured recipes are shared with visitors, creating an immersive experience that invites them to savour not just the cuisine but the essence of Ravello's local culture.

Ravello Reverie: Discovering Ravello's enchanted charms

Nestled on the Amalfi Coast, Ravello enchants visitors with its timeless beauty and a rich tapestry of landmarks that narrate the town's historical and cultural saga. From medieval marvels to botanical wonders, Ravello's landmarks stand as testaments to the town's enduring charm. Join us on a captivating exploration of Ravello's architectural splendour, where each landmark whispers stories of bygone eras and offers panoramic views that stir the soul.

Villa Cimbrone

Step into the enchanting realms of Villa Cimbrone, an exquisite estate dating back to the 11th century. The gardens, adorned with classical statues and flower-lined pathways, lead to the Terrace of Infinity-a vantage point offering breath-taking views of the Amalfi Coast. This iconic landmark seamlessly blends history, art and nature.

Villa Eva

Discover the elegant charm of Villa Eva, an aristocratic villa surrounded by enchanting gardens and adorned with neoclassical features. This landmark has witnessed centuries of cultural gatherings and retains an air of sophistication that reflects Ravello's historic grandeur.

San Giovanni del Toro

Uncover the mystique of San Giovanni del Toro, a medieval abbey with a storied past. This architectural gem boasts a blend of Romanesque and Moorish influences, creating a captivating atmosphere. Wander through its cloisters and explore the rich history that permeates the abbey's walls.

Auditorium Oscar Niemeyer

Step into modernity at the Auditorium Oscar Niemeyer, a contemporary cultural hub that pays homage to Ravello's artistic spirit. Designed by the renowned Brazilian architect, this landmark hosts concerts, exhibitions and events, adding a touch of modernity to Ravello's historic panorama.

Villa Rufolo

Embrace the allure of Villa Rufolo, a 13th-century estate that captures the essence of Ravello's aristocratic past. With its lush gardens and panoramic terraces overlooking the Tyrrhenian Sea, this landmark has inspired artists and writers for centuries. Wander through the ornate halls and vibrant gardens that once hosted Wagner's famous concerts during the Ravello Festival.

Chapel of Santa Maria dei Raccomandati

Visit the Chapel of Santa Maria dei Raccomandati, adorned with medieval frescoes. Tucked away in the heart of Ravello, this intimate chapel provides a quiet retreat, allowing visitors to admire the intricate artwork and sense the spiritual tranquillity within its walls.

Saint Francis Convent

Delve into the serenity of the Saint Francis Convent, a Franciscan monastery surrounded by tranquil gardens. The convent's simplicity and spiritual ambiance provide a peaceful retreat, inviting contemplation amidst Ravello's vibrant tapestry.

Ravello Art Gallery

Explore the Ravello Art Gallery, a cultural hub that showcases the town's contemporary artistic expressions. Nestled within the historic heart of Ravello, the gallery features a diverse collection of paintings, sculptures and installations, reflecting the town's ongoing commitment to artistic innovation.

Rufolo Tower

Ascend the Rufolo Tower, an ancient watchtower that once guarded Ravello against maritime threats. Today, it offers panoramic views of the Amalfi Coast and the Mediterranean Sea, making it a favoured spot for those seeking a mesmerizing perspective of Ravello's coastal landscape.

Ravello's landmarks stand as guardians of its rich history and captivating beauty. Each site tells a unique story, inviting visitors to traverse the epochs and bask in the timeless allure that defines this extraordinary town on the Amalfi Coast.

Hilltop harmony: Tasting Ravello's culinary melodies

In the heart of the Amalfi Coast, Ravello not only enchants with its breath-taking vistas but also entices the palate with a gastronomic symphony that celebrates the region's rich culinary heritage. From fresh seafood to handcrafted pastries, Ravello's culinary scene is a delightful fusion of tradition and innovation. Join us on a culinary journey through the town's charming streets, where each bite is a harmonious blend of flavours that captures the essence of coastal Italian cuisine.

Scialatielli alle Vongole

Indulge in the flavours of the sea with Scialatielli alle Vongole, a pasta dish that marries homemade ribbon-like pasta with tender clams. Bathed in a delicate white wine and garlic sauce, this dish exemplifies the simplicity and elegance of Ravello's coastal cuisine.

Ravello's Octopus Salad

Embark on a culinary adventure with Ravello's Octopus Salad, a refreshing and vibrant dish that combines tender octopus with crisp vegetables, drizzled in a citrus-infused dressing. This seafood medley captures the essence of Ravello's coastal location.

Risotto ai Frutti di Mare

Indulge in the decadence of Risotto ai Frutti di Mare, a seafood risotto that combines the freshest catch of the day with creamy Arborio rice. This dish encapsulates the essence of Ravello's commitment to using locally sourced ingredients.

Fiori di Zucca Ripieni

Experience the delicate flavours of Fiori di Zucca Ripieni, where zucchini flowers are stuffed with ricotta and herbs, then lightly battered and fried to golden perfection. This culinary masterpiece highlights the seasonal treasures of Ravello's gardens

Melanzane alla Parmigiana

Delight in the comforting layers of Melanzane alla Parmigiana, a classic dish featuring thinly sliced eggplant, rich tomato sauce and melted cheese. This savoury creation showcases the region's love for simple, yet profoundly flavourful, ingredients.

Sfogliatella Riccia

Indulge your sweet tooth with Sfogliatella Riccia, a pastry that marries layers of crisp, flaky dough with a sweet and citrus-infused ricotta filling. This iconic Neapolitan delight is a popular choice for those seeking a heavenly dessert experience in Ravello.

Caprese Salad

Experience the simplicity of Caprese Salad, a dish that celebrates the exquisite combination of fresh mozzarella, ripe tomatoes and fragrant basil, drizzled with extra virgin olive oil. This light and flavourful creation pays homage to the region's dedication to high-quality, local produce.

Amalfi Coast Gelato

Conclude your culinary journey with a scoop of Amalfi Coast Gelato, where the creamy, artisanal flavours capture the essence of the region. From classic pistachio to zesty lemon, each bite is a celebration of Italy's renowned gelato culture.

Gnocchi alla Sorrentina

Delight in the pillowy softness of Gnocchi alla Sorrentina, a dish that showcases potato dumplings bathed in tomato sauce, melted mozzarella and fresh basil. This comforting and flavoursome dish embodies the warmth and hospitality of Ravello's culinary tradition.

Ravello's culinary delights offer a feast for the senses, blending the finest local ingredients with time-honoured recipes. From seafood sensations to sweet indulgences, every bite in Ravello is a testament to the region's commitment to preserving its rich gastronomic heritage.

Echoes of elegance: Revealing Ravello's hidden gems

As you wander the charming streets of Ravello, beyond its renowned landmarks and bustling piazzas, you'll discover a collection of hidden gems that add an extra layer of enchantment to this coastal haven. These lesser-known treasures offer a glimpse into the intimate corners of Ravello, where local secrets and quiet wonders await. Join us on an exploration of Ravello's hidden gems, each with its unique story and charm, waiting to be uncovered by those who venture off the beaten path.

Via delle Sirene

Embark on a magical journey along Via delle Sirene, also known as the Mermaid's Path. This narrow, winding trail unveils breath-taking vistas and leads to hidden corners of Ravello. A haven for photography enthusiasts, this hidden gem promises glimpses of the coastline and the mesmerizing azure waters below.

Cimbrone Crypt

Step into the mysterious allure of the Cimbrone Crypt, an underground sanctuary beneath Villa Cimbrone. Rich in history and adorned with ancient artifacts, this hidden gem offers a fascinating glimpse into the past, showcasing the architectural intricacies and cryptic charm that lie beneath the surface.

Scala, Ravello's Sister Village

Escape to the adjacent village of Scala, Ravello's lesser-known sister. Tucked away in the hills, Scala exudes a quiet charm with its medieval architecture and authentic local life. Wander through its narrow streets, discover quaint chapels and experience the authentic, untarnished soul of this hidden gem.

Torre Maggiore

Uncover the secrets of Torre Maggiore, a medieval tower nestled away from the crowds. This hidden gem offers an opportunity to explore history up close, climb ancient stone steps and be rewarded with panoramic views of Ravello and its breath-taking surroundings.

Secret Beach Cove

Escape the bustling beaches and discover the Secret Beach Cove of Spiaggia del Furore. Accessible via a steep staircase, this hidden gem offers a secluded spot with crystal-clear waters, surrounded by dramatic cliffs. A retreat for those seeking a more private sun-soaked experience.

Ravello Jazz Festival's Venues

Immerse yourself in the soulful notes of the Ravello Jazz Festival, discovering its hidden venues tucked away in charming corners of the town. These intimate settings provide a unique and personal experience, where music lovers can enjoy world-class performances in a cosy and atmospheric ambiance.

Villa Maria Gardens

Escape to the secluded haven of Villa Maria Gardens, a verdant oasis tucked away from the main thoroughfares. This hidden gem invites you to stroll through manicured lawns, vibrant flowerbeds and secluded nooks, offering a tranquil retreat with stunning views of the Amalfi Coast. A serene paradise for those seeking respite from the bustling crowds.

Ravello's hidden gems unveil a side of the town reserved for the curious and adventurous. Beyond the well-trodden paths, these treasures add an extra layer of magic to your exploration, ensuring that every corner of Ravello holds surprises for those willing to seek them out.

Coastal tranquillity: Embracing outdoor adventures in Ravello's seaside sanctuary

Embrace the natural beauty of Ravello through a tapestry of outdoor activities that invite you to explore the region's breath-taking landscapes and immerse yourself in the coastal allure. From scenic walks along ancient paths to thrilling adventures on the azure waters of the Tyrrhenian Sea, Ravello offers an array of outdoor experiences that captivate the senses. Join us as we unfold the canvas of Ravello's outdoor delights, each stroke of nature's brush revealing a new and exhilarating adventure.

Path of the God's hike

Embark on the legendary Path of the God's hike, a trail that meanders along the rugged cliffs of the Amalfi Coast. Marvel at panoramic views of the sea and the coastline, with glimpses of picturesque villages below. This challenging yet rewarding trek is a must for nature enthusiasts seeking an unforgettable outdoor experience.

Boat excursion to Grotta dello Smeraldo

Sail into the enchanting emerald waters with a boat excursion to Grotta dello Smeraldo. Discover the hidden sea cave adorned with a spectrum of iridescent blue and green hues, creating a magical underwater world. This maritime adventure promises a refreshing and awe-inspiring connection with Ravello's coastal wonders.

Bike ride through lemon groves

Embark on a bike ride through the fragrant lemon groves that blanket the hills surrounding Ravello. Traverse scenic trails, passing by terraced orchards and quaint villages. This outdoor adventure provides a sensory journey, with the sweet scent of lemons accompanying you on your two-wheeled exploration.

Ravello concerts in the cloister

Experience the harmonious blend of music and nature with outdoor concerts in Ravello's historic cloisters. These open-air performances, often held in Villa Rufolo's gardens, allow you to revel in the sounds of classical and contemporary melodies while surrounded by the town's timeless charm.

Kayaking along the Amalfi Coast

Embark on a kayaking adventure along the Amalfi Coast, exploring hidden coves and pristine beaches. Paddle through the azure waters, with the dramatic coastline as your backdrop. This outdoor activity provides a unique perspective of Ravello's coastal beauty, promising an exhilarating and refreshing escape.

Sunset picnic in Minori
Savour the magic of Ravello's sunsets with a picnic in the charming seaside town of Minori. Find a cosy spot on the beach or cliffs, surrounded by the warm hues of the descending sun. This outdoor experience combines the delights of local cuisine with the breath-taking spectacle of twilight over the Tyrrhenian Sea.

Stand-Up Paddleboarding in Atrani

Glide across the gentle waves of the Tyrrhenian Sea with stand-up paddleboarding in the quaint village of Atrani. Enjoy the tranquillity of the sea as you navigate along the coastline, taking in the stunning views of Ravello from a unique vantage point.

Yoga retreats in nature

Find harmony and tranquillity through outdoor yoga retreats set against the backdrop of Ravello's natural wonders. Engage in mindful practices surrounded by lush landscapes, allowing the serene ambiance to deepen your connection with both body and soul.

Scenic drive along the Amalfi Coast

Embark on a scenic drive along the Amalfi Coast, winding through picturesque cliffs and charming villages. Whether self-driving or opting for a chauffeured experience, this outdoor activity offers breath-taking panoramas at every turn, revealing the timeless beauty of Ravello and its coastal neighbours.

Ravello's outdoor activities paint a vivid portrait of the region's natural splendour. Whether you're seeking adrenaline-pumping adventures or serene moments of reflection, Ravello invites you to explore its outdoor canvas, where every stroke is a celebration of the beauty that surrounds this enchanting town.

Enchantment in Ravello: Exploring local traditions

Ravello, steeped in history and vibrant cultural traditions, comes alive throughout the year with a tapestry of local celebrations and festivals. These events not only honour the town's rich heritage but also provide a unique opportunity for visitors to immerse themselves in the spirited essence of Ravello. From religious processions to music and arts festivals, each tradition reflects the warmth and authenticity of the local community. Join us as we unravel the threads of Ravello's cultural fabric, exploring the traditions and festivals that paint the town with a lively and colourful brush.

Ravello Festival (July - August)

At the heart of Ravello's cultural calendar is the renowned Ravello Festival. Held in the picturesque settings of Villa Rufolo and Villa Cimbrone, this internationally acclaimed event showcases classical music, dance and contemporary performances. The festival, which has graced Ravello since 1953, transforms the town into a cultural haven, attracting artists and enthusiasts from around the world.

Good Friday Procession (April)

Experience the solemn beauty of Ravello during the Good Friday Procession, a deeply rooted religious tradition. The procession winds its way through the town's historic streets, commemorating the Passion of Christ. Adorned with statues, crucifixes and religious symbols, the procession is a poignant expression of faith and community solidarity.

Santa Maria a Gradillo Feast (September)

Join the joyful celebrations of the Santa Maria a Gradillo Feast, an event that pays homage to Ravello's patron saint. The festivities include religious ceremonies, processions and a lively market, where locals and visitors alike come together to celebrate the town's spiritual heritage with music, dance and traditional food.

Ravello Concerts in the Cloisters (July - September)

Beyond the Ravello Festival, the town's historic cloisters host enchanting open-air concerts throughout the year. These musical gatherings, set against the backdrop of ancient architecture, provide an intimate and immersive experience, connecting attendees with the timeless charm of Ravello's cultural heritage.

Corpus Domini Procession (June)

Participate in the Corpus Domini Procession, an ancient religious tradition that takes place in Ravello. The procession features the Eucharist carried through the streets adorned with intricate flower carpets, creating a breath-taking visual spectacle. This sacred event is a testament to the deep-rooted religious heritage of the town.

Amalfi Coast Film Festival (June)

Celebrate the art of cinema against the stunning backdrop of the Amalfi Coast during the Amalfi Coast Film Festival. Ravello becomes a cinematic canvas, hosting film screenings, discussions and cultural events that bring together filmmakers, enthusiasts and the local community.

Ravello Prize Award Ceremony (September)

Celebrate artistic excellence during the Ravello Prize Award Ceremony. This prestigious event honours individuals who have made significant contributions to the fields of arts, literature and science. The award ceremony, often accompanied by cultural events, adds an intellectual and inspirational dimension to Ravello's cultural calendar.

Ravello Short Film Festival (November)

Embrace the cinematic arts with the Ravello Short Film Festival. This emerging event showcases short films from local and international filmmakers, fostering a dynamic platform for storytelling and artistic expression. The festival provides an engaging and accessible avenue for film enthusiasts to discover new voices in the world of cinema.

Tarantella Dance Nights (June - August)

Step into the rhythmic world of the Tarantella during lively dance nights held in Ravello. This traditional Italian folk dance, characterized by energetic and intricate movements, becomes a communal celebration where locals and visitors come together to revel in the joyous spirit of this cultural expression.

Ravello's local traditions and festivals form an integral part of the town's identity, offering a glimpse into its cultural soul. Whether attending internationally acclaimed performances or participating in centuries-old religious processions, visitors are invited to become a part of Ravello's vibrant tapestry of traditions and celebrations.

Mediterranean memoirs: Insider's guide to exploring Ravello

As you prepare to embark on a journey to the captivating town of Ravello, nestled along the Amalfi Coast, a tapestry of experiences awaits you. To ensure your visit is seamless and filled with delightful discoveries, here are invaluable travel tips that unveil the nuances of this enchanting destination. From navigating the scenic landscapes to savouring local flavours, these insights will enhance your Ravello sojourn, allowing you to immerse yourself in the timeless beauty and cultural richness that define this Italian gem.

Seasonal splendour

Timing is key when planning your Ravello adventure. The summer months (June to August) bring vibrant festivals and open-air concerts, while the quieter spring and fall seasons offer a more serene experience with milder temperatures and blooming landscapes. Consider your preferred atmosphere and activities when choosing the perfect time to visit.

Amalfi Coast transportation tactics

The Amalfi Coast's winding roads can be both charming and challenging. Consider hiring a local driver or using public transportation to navigate the picturesque yet narrow coastal routes. Boats also provide a scenic alternative for reaching nearby destinations.

Stroll-friendly footwear

Ravello's charm lies in its cobbled streets and terraced landscapes. Opt for comfortable, sturdy footwear as you explore the town's alleys and stairs. Your feet will thank you for the support during leisurely walks through gardens and historic sites.

Villa exploration etiquette

Ravello boasts historic villas like Villa Rufolo and Villa Cimbrone, each with its unique charm. Respectful attire, especially if you plan to explore gardens and cloisters, ensures a smooth entry. Remember to check opening hours and any specific guidelines before visiting.

Cash and Card considerations

While many places in Ravello accept cards, it's wise to have some cash on hand for smaller establishments or markets. Inform your bank about your travel dates to avoid any issues with card transactions and use ATMs in the town for convenient currency exchange.

Cultural dress code

Ravello, like many Italian towns, appreciates modest attire when visiting religious sites or attending cultural events. A light shawl or scarf can be handy for covering shoulders when needed. Embrace a touch of elegance that aligns with the local aesthetic.

Hiking essentials

If you plan to explore Ravello's scenic hiking trails, pack essentials like comfortable hiking shoes, a refillable water bottle and sunscreen. The Path of the Gods and other routes offer breath-taking views, so be prepared for an immersive and rewarding experience.

Language learning

While many locals in Ravello understand English, learning a few basic Italian phrases can enhance your experience and show appreciation for the local culture. A warm 'Buongiorno' or 'Grazie' can go a long way.

Relaxation rituals

Amidst exploration, prioritize moments of relaxation. Whether it's sipping espresso in a charming café, enjoying a leisurely meal with a view, or partaking in a seaside sunset, allow yourself the luxury of absorbing Ravello's tranquillity.

Event calendar awareness

Before your visit, check Ravello's event calendar for festivals, concerts and cultural happenings. Attending these local events not only adds vibrancy to your trip but also provides insight into the community's spirit.

Camera in hand, battery in check

Ravello's vistas are postcard-perfect, so ensure your camera is ready to capture every picturesque moment. Carry spare batteries or a portable charger to keep your devices powered throughout the day.

Respectful photography practices

While capturing memories, be mindful of your surroundings, especially in churches and private areas. Some places may have restrictions on photography, so always ask for permission when in doubt.

Weather-ready wardrobe

Ravello's climate can vary, so pack layers to adapt to changing weather. A light jacket for cooler evenings and comfortable attire for warmer days will keep you prepared for any climate surprises.

Transport tips from Naples

If arriving from Naples, consider the scenic ferry ride from Salerno or Amalfi for a unique approach to Ravello. Ferries provide stunning views of the coastline and offer a relaxed introduction to your Amalfi Coast adventure.

Navigating Ravello becomes a joy with these travel tips, ensuring your journey is filled with seamless moments and unforgettable discoveries. Embrace the charm, culture and warmth of this Amalfi Coast gem as you embark on an enchanting exploration of Ravello's timeless allure.

Symphony of serenity: Concluding the adventure with harmonious reflections

In these closing reflections, Ravello emerges not just as a destination but as an enduring muse for artists, musicians and wanderers alike. Its local culture, celebrated through the Ravello Festival and artisanal traditions, adds depth to the town's charm. The warmth of hospitality and the flavours of traditional cuisine linger in the memory, inviting a return to this cliffside haven.

As the Mediterranean sun sets over the Tyrrhenian Sea, casting its warm glow on Ravello's historic villas and charming piazzas, one can't help but be captivated by the timeless allure of this Italian gem. In the spirit of Ravello's enduring beauty, may the memories forged within its embrace be cherished, echoing the sentiment that this cliffside retreat is not merely a place but a timeless experience etched into the hearts of all who have wandered its storied streets.

Sorrento-Sunshine escape on the Mediterranean

Sorrentine serenade: A prelude to enchanted clifftops

Nestled atop the cliffs overlooking the Bay of Naples, Sorrento unfolds as a captivating tale of ancient charm and contemporary allure and is located approximately 50 kilometres south of Naples and about 25 kilometres southwest of Positano. This idyllic town, perched on the Sorrentine Peninsula along the southwestern coast of Italy, has beckoned travellers for centuries with its panoramic views of the Tyrrhenian Sea, the scent of citrus groves in the air and a rich tapestry of history that weaves seamlessly into its cobblestone streets. Renowned for its dramatic cliffs, Sorrento serves as a gateway to the Amalfi Coast, offering a tantalizing blend of Mediterranean splendour and Italian sophistication. Known for its stunning views of Mount Vesuvius and the Isle of Capri, Sorrento is a popular destination for travellers seeking sun, sea and relaxation. Sorrento, a town overlooking the Bay of Naples in southern Italy, is situated at a relatively low altitude. The town itself is at sea level, but some nearby areas may have slightly higher elevations.

The town's name is synonymous with the sweet-scented lemon orchards that carpet the surrounding hills, providing the key ingredient for the famous Limoncello liqueur. As one strolls through the labyrinthine streets of Sorrento, lined with pastel-coloured buildings and boutique shops, it becomes evident that this town is a seamless blend of the timeless and the contemporary-a destination where tradition and modernity converge to create an enchanting atmosphere that leaves an indelible mark on those fortunate enough to explore its treasures.

Clifftop chronicles: Sorrento's time-imbued tale

Sorrento's historical significance is deeply rooted in the layers of civilizations that have left their indelible mark on this enchanting coastal town. Tracing its origins back to ancient times, Sorrento was a favoured destination for the Greeks who established colonies along the southern Italian coast. With the rise of the Roman Empire, Sorrento became a prestigious resort, attracting emperors and aristocrats drawn to its scenic landscapes and therapeutic sea baths. The town continued to flourish through the Middle Ages, experiencing the influences of Norman, Byzantine and Arab cultures that shaped its unique character.

Throughout history, Sorrento has borne witness to a tapestry of events, from maritime trade and the struggles for control over the Mediterranean to the influx of artistic and intellectual movements during the Renaissance. The historic heart of Sorrento, characterized by its medieval architecture and charming piazzas, tells the tales of ancient craftsmanship and maritime prowess. Notable landmarks, such as the 15th-century Sedil Dominova and the Cathedral of Sorrento, stand as architectural testaments to the town's rich heritage. As one explores Sorrento's historical sites, including the Roman ruins of Villa Pollio and the charming fishing village of Marina Grande, it becomes evident that this town is a living museum, where each cobblestone and weathered stone wall whispers stories of centuries gone by.

Sun-kissed shores: Exploring Sorrento's coastal paradise

Sorrento's local culture is a vibrant tapestry woven with traditions, flavours and a warm sense of hospitality. Rooted in a deep connection to the surrounding land and sea, the residents of Sorrento, known as Surrentini, take immense pride in preserving their cultural heritage. The town's unique blend of influences-from Greek and Roman to Norman and Byzantine-has given rise to a distinctive way of life that embraces both historical traditions and modern sensibilities.

Traditional dishes showcase the flavours of the Mediterranean, with fresh seafood, olive oil and aromatic herbs taking centre stage. The local craftsmanship is another pillar of Sorrento's culture, with intricate woodwork, inlaid marquetry (intarsia)and handmade ceramics adorning the shops and artisan workshops. The town's commitment to the arts is also evident in its annual events and festivals, celebrating everything from music and literature to the revered patron saint, Sant'Antonino. Sorrento's local culture invites visitors to savour the nuances of daily life, from leisurely strolls along the seaside promenades to engaging with artisans in their studios, providing an authentic and immersive experience in this coastal haven.

Cliffside chronicles: Unveiling the enchanted tale of Sorrento's coast

Sorrento, perched atop the cliffs overlooking the Bay of Naples, is a treasure trove of history and natural splendour. As you wander through its narrow streets and gaze out at the azure waters, the town's landmarks stand as testaments to its rich past and enduring charm. From ancient marvels to panoramic viewpoints, Sorrento's landmarks beckon travellers to delve into its captivating narrative. Here's a curated guide to the town's most captivating points of interest, each offering a unique perspective on Sorrento's allure.

Piazza Tasso

Nestled at the heart of Sorrento, Piazza Tasso is a bustling square named after the renowned poet Torquato Tasso, born in the town. The lively atmosphere, surrounded by cafes and shops, makes it an ideal starting point for exploration. Take a moment to appreciate the statue of Torquato Tasso while soaking in the energy of this central hub.

Marina Piccola

Discover the charm of Marina Piccola, Sorrento's small but inviting harbour. Watch as fishing boats bob on the gentle waves and enjoy the vibrant colours of the waterfront. This is also the departure point for boat trips to the nearby islands of Capri and Ischia.

Museo Correale di Terranova

Delve into Sorrento's artistic heritage at the Museo Correale di Terranova. Housed in a neoclassical villa, the museum features an impressive collection of paintings, decorative arts and archaeological finds, offering a comprehensive view of Sorrento's cultural evolution.

Sorrento Cathedral

Dedicated to Saints Philip and James, the Sorrento Cathedral, or Duomo, is a masterpiece of religious architecture. Its stunning facade features intricate carvings and the interior boasts remarkable frescoes and a crypt that houses the remains of Saint Antonino, the town's patron saint.

Via San Cesareo

Stroll along Via San Cesareo, Sorrento's main shopping street. Lined with boutiques, cafes and artisan shops, it's a vibrant thoroughfare that captures the essence of the town's bustling activity.

Villa Angelina

For panoramic views of the Sorrento coastline, visit Villa Angelina. This elegant villa, adorned with lush gardens and statues, offers an elevated perspective of the Bay of Naples and Mount Vesuvius. It's a serene spot to appreciate the beauty of the surrounding landscapes.

Villa Pollio

Step back in time at Villa Pollio, an ancient Roman villa located in the Piano di Sorrento area. This archaeological site reveals well-preserved frescoes and structures, offering a fascinating glimpse into the opulent lifestyle of the Roman elite.

Bagni della Regina Giovanna

Escape to the natural beauty of Bagni della Regina Giovanna, near Sorrento. This secluded cove, surrounded by rocky cliffs, is believed to be the private bathhouse of Queen Joanna II. Take a dip in the crystal-clear waters and absorb the tranquil atmosphere of this picturesque coastal retreat.

Lemon Groves of Sorrento

Explore the fragrant lemon groves that blanket the hillsides of Sorrento. Known for their production of Limoncello, these terraced orchards showcase the town's agrarian traditions. Many local farms offer tours, allowing visitors to learn about the cultivation of Sorrento's prized lemons.

Tasso Theatre

Immerse yourself in Sorrento's cultural scene at the Tasso Theatre. This historic venue hosts a variety of performances, including plays, concerts and traditional Neapolitan shows. Attend a live performance to appreciate the town's artistic vibrancy.

Ancient Walls of Sorrento

Discover remnants of Sorrento's ancient fortifications by exploring the town's walls. These historic structures, including the Gate of Parsano and the Bastion of St. Antonino, offer glimpses into Sorrento's medieval past.

Antico Bagno Stabilimento Balneare

Relax at the Antico Bagno Stabilimento Balneare, one of Sorrento's historic bathing establishments. Dating back to the early 20th century, it provides a nostalgic glimpse into the town's seaside leisure culture.

Villa Comunale

For panoramic views and serene moments, head to Villa Comunale. Overlooking the fishing village of Marina Grande, this park offers lush greenery and charming walkways. The sight of Mount Vesuvius across the Bay of Naples adds to the allure of this scenic retreat.

Sorrento's landmarks weave a tapestry of history, culture and natural beauty, inviting visitors to unravel the layers of its enchanting story. Each site contributes to the unique character of this coastal haven, making it a destination where the past and present seamlessly intertwine.

Mediterranean melodies: Savouring Sorrento's culinary harmony

Sorrento, perched on the sun-kissed cliffs overlooking the Bay of Naples, not only captivates with its stunning vistas but also enchants the palate with a culinary repertoire deeply rooted in its coastal heritage. From the freshest catch of the Mediterranean to the citrusy zing of Sorrento lemons, each dish is a celebration of local ingredients and time-honoured recipes. Join us on a gastronomic journey through Sorrento's culinary delights, where every bite is a sensory voyage into the heart of this enchanting coastal town.

Linguine alle Vongole

Delight in the simplicity and freshness of Linguine alle Vongole. This classic dish features perfectly cooked linguine entwined with succulent clams, garlic, fresh parsley and a drizzle of extra-virgin olive oil. The flavours mirror the sea breeze that caresses Sorrento's shores, providing a true taste of the Mediterranean.

Gnocchi alla Sorrentina

Indulge in the comforting embrace of Gnocchi alla Sorrentina. Soft potato dumplings are bathed in a luscious tomato sauce, adorned with melted mozzarella and baked to golden perfection. This dish embodies the warmth of Sorrento's kitchens, offering a hearty and satisfying culinary experience.

Risotto al Limone

Experience the zesty elegance of Risotto al Limone, a dish that showcases Sorrento's famed lemons. Arborio rice is cooked to creamy perfection, infused with the citrusy brightness of Sorrento lemons and finished with Parmesan cheese. This culinary masterpiece harmonizes the town's citrus groves with the richness of Italian risotto.

Baba au Rhum

Indulge your sweet tooth with a decadent Baba au Rhum, a rum-soaked sponge cake infused with citrus zest and served with a dollop of freshly whipped cream. This irresistible dessert is a testament to Sorrento's love affair with lemons and is the perfect way to end a memorable meal on a sweet note.

Scialatielli ai Frutti di Mare

Embark on a seafood extravaganza with Scialatielli ai Frutti di Mare. This pasta dish features broad ribbons of Scialatielli intertwined with an array of fresh seafood, from tender calamari to plump shrimp, all bathed in a fragrant tomato and white wine sauce. It's a seafood lover's dream on a plate.

Melanzane alla Parmigiana

Savour the layers of flavour in Melanzane alla Parmigiana. Thin slices of eggplant are delicately fried, layered with rich tomato sauce, mozzarella and Parmesan cheese, then baked to golden perfection. This dish embodies the heartiness and depth of Sorrento's traditional cuisine.

Sfogliatella

Indulge your sweet tooth with Sfogliatella, a classic Neapolitan pastry that has found a cherished home in Sorrento. Layers of thin pastry dough envelop a filling of ricotta, citrus zest and sugar, creating a flaky, sweet and utterly irresistible treat.

Limoncello

Conclude your culinary journey with Sorrento's signature digestif-Limoncello. This vibrant lemon liqueur, crafted from the renowned Sorrento lemons, offers a refreshing and tangy finale to your meal. Sip it slowly and let the essence of Sorrento linger on your palate.

Torta Caprese

Indulge in the chocolatey decadence of Torta Caprese. This flourless chocolate and almond cake, dusted with powdered sugar, showcases the region's commitment to simple yet indulgent desserts. Each bite is a celebration of Sorrento's sweet traditions.

Sorrento's culinary tapestry weaves together the freshest ingredients, time-honoured techniques and a dash of Mediterranean sunshine, creating a symphony of flavours that dance on the taste buds-a true feast for the senses in this coastal haven.

Hidden havens: Sorrento's Treasures await discovery

Beyond the sun-soaked streets and popular landmarks, Sorrento harbours a secret world of hidden gems waiting to be discovered. These tucked-away treasures reveal the town's authentic charm, offering a glimpse into its lesser-explored facets. Join us on a journey through Sorrento's hidden gems, where each locale tells a story and every corner holds a delightful surprise, enriching your experience in this coastal paradise.

Museo Bottega della Tarsia Lignea

Unearth the Museo Bottega della Tarsia Lignea, a museum dedicated to the intricate art of wood inlay. This hidden gem showcases masterpieces crafted by local artisans, providing insight into the intricate techniques that have adorned Sorrento's wooden creations for generations.

Parsano Gate

Step through the historic Parsano Gate, a lesser-known entrance to Sorrento's medieval walls. This well-preserved gate invites you to wander off the beaten path and explore the quieter side of the town, offering a glimpse into its ancient fortifications.

Chiesa di Santa Maria delle Grazie

Find tranquillity in the Chiesa di Santa Maria delle Grazie, a hidden church away from the bustling centre. Adorned with beautiful frescoes, this lesser-visited gem provides a serene space for reflection amidst the rich religious history of Sorrento.

Vallone dei Mulini Profondo

Descend into the Vallone dei Mulini Profondo, an extension of the more well-known Valley of the Mills. This secluded oasis unveils the remnants of ancient mills surrounded by lush greenery. The atmospheric ambiance and the echoes of Sorrento's industrial past make it a tranquil escape from the bustling streets.

Antico Bagno Stabilimento Balneare

Relax at the Antico Bagno Stabilimento Balneare, a historic bathing establishment that harks back to the early 20th century. Tucked away from the main crowds, this charming spot allows you to experience Sorrento's seaside leisure culture in a more intimate setting.

Giardino della Minerva

Wander through the Giardino della Minerva, a hidden botanical garden that showcases medicinal plants and herbs. This aromatic haven provides a peaceful escape and a glimpse into Sorrento's historical use of herbs for both culinary and medicinal purposes.

Villa La Ruota

Embark on a journey to Villa La Ruota, a hidden villa that boasts panoramic views of the Bay of Naples. Tucked away in the hills, this vantage point offers a quieter retreat, allowing you to soak in the beauty of Sorrento's coastline away from the crowds.

Fontana di Sant'Antonino

Discover the Fontana di Sant'Antonino, a charming fountain tucked in a quiet corner of Sorrento. This hidden gem, dedicated to the town's patron saint, invites moments of reflection and respite amid the town's vibrant energy.

Chiesa di San Francesco Cloister

Discover the serene Cloister of Chiesa di San Francesco, a hidden haven attached to the Church of San Francesco. The cloister's tranquil atmosphere, adorned with graceful arches and a central garden, offers a peaceful retreat and a glimpse into Sorrento's religious history.

Sorrento's hidden gems promise enchanting surprises for those willing to venture off the well-trodden path. Each discovery unveils a new layer of the town's history, culture and natural beauty, inviting you to experience Sorrento in its most authentic and undiscovered form.

Seaside serenade: Outdoor pursuits in Sorrento's scenic landscape

Sorrento, nestled between the azure waters of the Tyrrhenian Sea and the lush hills of the Sorrentine Peninsula, is a haven for outdoor enthusiasts seeking both tranquillity and adrenaline-fueled escapades. Explore the natural wonders that surround this coastal gem, from leisurely strolls along cliffside paths to thrilling sea adventures. Join us on a journey through Sorrento's outdoor realm, where every activity is a harmonious blend of sun-soaked landscapes and exhilarating experiences.

Hiking the path of the Gods

Embark on a celestial journey by hiking the Path of the Gods. This panoramic trail winds through the cliffs of the Sorrentine Peninsula, offering awe-inspiring views of the Amalfi Coast and the Gulf of Salerno. A trek along this celestial path is a testament to Sorrento's breath-taking natural beauty.

Kayaking along the Coast

Paddle into the azure embrace of the Tyrrhenian Sea with a kayaking adventure along Sorrento's coastline. Glide past hidden coves, sea caves and dramatic cliffs, immersing yourself in the coastal splendour that unfolds around every bend.

Mountain biking in the hills

Saddle up for a mountain biking expedition through the undulating hills surrounding Sorrento. Explore charming villages, lemon groves and ancient ruins, feeling the exhilaration of navigating diverse terrains while taking in the scenic landscapes that define the region.

Snorkelling in Marina Grande

Dive into the crystal-clear waters of Marina Grande for a snorkelling adventure. Explore the vibrant marine life beneath the surface, from colourful fish to submerged rock formations. The tranquil bay provides an ideal setting for both novice and experienced snorkelers.

Boat excursion to Capri

Set sail on a boat excursion to the enchanting island of Capri. Cruise along the Sorrentine Coast, revelling in the views of hidden grottoes and rugged cliffs, before reaching Capri's iconic Blue Grotto and Faraglioni Rocks.

Sunset at Punta Campanella

Witness the magical transformation of the sky as you hike to Punta Campanella to catch the sunset. This strategic viewpoint offers an unobstructed panorama of the sun dipping below the horizon, casting hues of gold and pink over the Gulf of Naples.

Picnicking in Villa Comunale

Enjoy an alfresco feast in Villa Comunale, Sorrento's cliffside park. Pack a picnic and revel in the Mediterranean breeze as you relax amidst flower-lined pathways and stunning views of the Bay of Naples.

Yoga on the terrace

Find serenity with an outdoor yoga session on one of Sorrento's panoramic terraces. Whether at sunrise or under the moonlight, practicing yoga amid the natural beauty of the coast rejuvenates both body and spirit.

Sorrento's outdoor activities offer a symphony of experiences, inviting you to immerse yourself in the region's natural wonders and adventurous spirit. From coastal explorations to hillside escapades, every outdoor pursuit in Sorrento unveils a new layer of its captivating allure.

Majestic mosaics: Sorrento's opulent tapestry of traditions

Sorrento, with its deep-rooted cultural heritage, comes alive throughout the year with a tapestry of local traditions and vibrant festivals. From religious processions echoing through ancient streets to lively celebrations that honour the town's unique identity, Sorrento invites you to immerse yourself in its rich cultural tapestry. Join us as we delve into the heart of Sorrento's traditions and festivals, where each event is a captivating expression of the town's history, spirituality and joyful spirit.

Feast of Sant'Antonino (February)

Celebrate Sorrento's patron saint during the Feast of Sant'Antonino. The town comes alive with processions, religious ceremonies and a lively atmosphere. Join locals in honouring St. Antonino, the protector of Sorrento, with parades, music and traditional performances.

Sorrento film festival (September)

Immerse yourself in the cinematic arts during the Sorrento Film Festival. This annual event showcases a curated selection of national and international films, bringing together filmmakers, artists and cinema enthusiasts. It's a cultural celebration that adds a modern touch to Sorrento's vibrant calendar.

Santa Lucia festival (December)

Participate in the Santa Lucia Festival, a celebration of light and devotion. The festival honours St. Lucia, the patron saint of sight, with a candle-lit procession through the streets, creating a magical ambiance that reflects the spiritual essence of Sorrento.

Lemon festival (July)

Embrace the zesty spirit of Sorrento during the Lemon Festival, an annual extravaganza that pays homage to the town's iconic lemons. Streets burst with vibrant citrus displays, parades and culinary events, showcasing the integral role lemons play in Sorrento's culture.

Sorrento Jazz festival (September)

Groove to the rhythms of jazz at the Sorrento Jazz Festival. This musical extravaganza features international and local jazz artists, creating an electrifying atmosphere in charming venues across Sorrento. Immerse yourself in the soulful notes that echo through the coastal town.

Sorrento summer of music (July - August)

Savour the sounds of classical music during the Sorrento Summer of Music. This festival, held in historic venues like the Cloister of San Francesco, showcases performances by renowned musicians, creating an enchanting cultural experience amid Sorrento's timeless beauty.

Tarantella dance festival (August)

Feel the rhythm of Sorrento's traditional Tarantella dance during the Tarantella Dance Festival. This lively event features performances by local dance troupes, celebrating the region's folk-dance heritage. Join in the festivities to experience the joyous energy of Tarantella.

Festival of grapes and wine (September)

Raise a glass to Sorrento's winemaking heritage during the Festival of Grapes and Wine. This event celebrates the harvest season with wine tastings, vineyard tours and cultural performances. It's a delightful opportunity to savour the flavours of Sorrento's local wines.

Sorrento's traditions and festivals offer a captivating journey into the heart of the town's cultural legacy. Whether immersed in religious fervour, dancing to folk tunes, or indulging in citrus celebrations, each event adds a vibrant thread to the fabric of Sorrento's cultural tapestry.

Sorrento serenity: Navigating coastal bliss with insider wisdom

Sorrento, with its sun-kissed cliffs, historic charm, and vibrant cultural scene, beckons travellers seeking a taste of coastal Italian paradise. To ensure your journey through Sorrento is seamless and richly rewarding, here are some insider travel tips. From navigating local customs to savouring culinary delights, let these recommendations be your compass for an unforgettable Sorrentine adventure.

Getting around

Explore Sorrento's enchanting streets on foot. The town is compact, making it ideal for leisurely strolls. If venturing beyond, use the efficient Circumvesuviana train or hop on a local bus to reach nearby destinations like Positano or Amalfi.

Best Time to Visit

Plan your visit between April and October for warm weather and a vibrant atmosphere. While the summer months are popular, consider the shoulder seasons of spring and fall for pleasant temperatures and fewer crowds.

Local Etiquette

Embrace the Italian way of life by engaging with locals. A simple 'Buongiorno' and a smile go a long way. Respectful attire is appreciated, especially when visiting churches or attending traditional events.

Lemon Everything

Indulge in Sorrento's love affair with lemons. Try limoncello, lemon-flavored gelato and lemon-infused dishes. Visit a local lemon grove for a first-hand experience of the citrus culture.

Booking Accommodations

Secure accommodations with breath-taking sea views. Many hotels and villas perch on cliffs, offering panoramic vistas of the Bay of Naples. Book in advance, especially during the peak season.

Exploring the Amalfi Coast

Take day trips to neighbouring gems like Positano, Amalfi and Ravello. Boats and buses provide scenic routes along the stunning Amalfi Coast, revealing picturesque landscapes at every turn.

Local Markets and Shops

Wander through Sorrento's markets, such as Piazza Tasso, to experience the lively atmosphere and shop for local products. Explore boutique stores for handmade crafts, ceramics and souvenirs.

Respect Siesta Time

Adapt to the local rhythm by observing siesta time. Many shops and businesses close during the early afternoon, allowing locals to enjoy a leisurely break. Plan accordingly to avoid disappointment.

Learn Basic Italian Phrases

Enhance your experience by learning a few basic Italian phrases. While many locals speak English, making an effort to communicate in Italian is appreciated and adds a personal touch to your interactions.

Reserve Excursions in Advance

For popular attractions and tours, such as boat trips to Capri or guided visits to historical sites, it's advisable to book in advance, ensuring you secure your spot and avoid disappointment.

Sorrento, with its captivating blend of history, culture and natural beauty, awaits your exploration. These travel tips are your key to unlocking the secrets of Sorrento, ensuring that every moment is filled with enchantment and unforgettable experiences.

Vesuvian verse: Reflecting on the Sorrento odyssey with poetic musings

In our closing reflections, Sorrento emerges not just as a destination but as a sensory journey-where the aroma of citrus groves mingles with the salty breeze of the Tyrrhenian Sea and the echoes of history resonate through cobblestone alleys. Its local culture, a vibrant mosaic of culinary delights, artisanal crafts and warm hospitality, beckons travellers to immerse themselves in the daily rhythms of Sorrento life.

Whether indulging in the flavours of Limoncello, admiring the craftsmanship of local artisans, or simply gazing at the sunset over the Bay of Naples, Sorrento invites a connection that transcends the temporal, leaving an enduring impression that echoes long after the journey ends. In the spirit of Sorrento's timeless charm, may the memories forged within its embrace linger as a cherished treasure for those fortunate enough to have experienced the magic of this captivating town.

Savoca: An enigma in every stone

Sicilian serenade: Prelude to Savoca's timeless tapestry

Nestled among the sun-drenched hills of Sicily, Savoca stands as a timeless oasis, beckoning travellers with its rich history, cultural tapestry and panoramic views of the Tyrrhenian Sea. Savoca, is located approximately 40 kilometres northeast of Messina and about 20 kilometres southwest of Taormina. As you step into this medieval jewel, the air is infused with the aroma of citrus groves and the cobblestone streets lead you through a labyrinth of historical wonders. Perched at an altitude of approximately 300 meters above sea level, Savoca offers stunning panoramic vistas of the surrounding countryside and coastline, making it a memorable destination for history buffs and nature lovers alike. Immortalized by its appearance in Francis Ford Coppola's 'The Godfather', Savoca is more than a cinematic backdrop-it's a living testament to Sicily's enduring charm. The medieval architecture, ancient churches and the remnants of Norman castles unfold like chapters in a captivating novel, inviting you to traverse the pages of history within the embrace of this Sicilian enclave.

Savoca's introduction is an invitation to embark on a journey through Sicily's past-a journey where time seems to stand still and every stone whispers tales of bygone eras. The medieval streets, flanked by stone houses adorned with bougainvillea, reveal the town's architectural prowess, while the panoramic vistas from the hilltops offer a breath-taking panorama of the Tyrrhenian coastline. As you explore the Church of San Michele, the Capuchin Monastery and the ancient Norman castle, Savoca's allure extends beyond its cinematic fame. It's a prelude to a Sicilian odyssey, where the echoes of antiquity harmonize with the coastal rhythms, setting the stage for a profound exploration of Savoca's cultural treasures.

Cultural resonance: Savoca's time-weathered tapestry

Savoca boasts a historical significance that transcends time. With origins dating back to ancient civilizations, the town stands as a testament to the enduring legacy of Sicily. Traversing its cobblestone streets, visitors encounter architectural marvels, such as the medieval Church of San Michele and the remnants of the Norman castle, each echoing the whispers of Greek, Roman and medieval influences. Savoca's historical tapestry, woven with the threads of diverse cultures and centuries-old traditions, invites exploration and offers a captivating glimpse into Sicily's intricate past.

Savoca's historical significance unfolds like chapters in a captivating novel, each era leaving its mark on the town's identity. From the Greek and Roman periods to medieval times, Savoca's landscape tells the story of ancient civilizations that once thrived on these sun-kissed hills. The imposing ruins of the Normanno castle and the intricate architecture of the Church of San Michele stand as living monuments, preserving the tales of conquests, cultural exchanges and the enduring spirit of Sicily. As you explore Savoca's winding streets, you step into a living history book where the layers of legacy await discovery, inviting you to unravel the secrets of this timeless Sicilian enclave.

Savoca serenade: Discovering Sicily's timeless charm

Savoca, a small Sicilian town perched on the hillside, emanates a profound cultural resonance that transcends its quaint exterior. Enveloped in the warmth of traditional Sicilian hospitality, Savoca welcomes visitors to partake in a lifestyle steeped in authenticity. The locals, proud custodians of their heritage, breathe life into the town's cultural identity through vibrant celebrations, artisanal crafts and a culinary tradition that mirrors Sicily's flavourful history. From lively festivals that pulse through the cobblestone streets to the intimate gatherings at family-run trattorias, Savoca invites travellers to immerse themselves in a Sicilian symphony-a harmonious blend of history, art and the enduring spirit of community.

Savoca's local culture finds expression in its artisanal crafts and gastronomic delights. The town is renowned for its skilled artisans who carry forward age-old traditions, producing intricate ceramics, handwoven textiles and delicate lacework that reflect the artistry of generations past. Culinary enthusiasts are in for a treat as Savoca showcases Sicilian cuisine at its finest. From aromatic citrus groves that perfume the air to trattorias serving time-honoured recipes, visitors can savour the flavours of Sicily, experiencing the cultural tapestry woven into every dish. In Savoca, the vibrant hues of local festivals, the skilful hands of artisans and the aromas wafting from kitchen windows converge, offering an authentic immersion into the heart of Sicilian culture.

Historical hideaway: Exploring Savoca's timeless treasures

Perched atop the hills of Sicily, the medieval town of Savoca enchants visitors with its timeless allure and historical charm. Far from the bustling crowds, this hidden gem boasts a rich tapestry of landmarks and points of interest that narrate the story of its storied past. From ancient churches to cinematic settings, each corner of Savoca unveils a piece of its fascinating history and cultural heritage. Let us embark on a journey through the cobbled streets and ancient alleys to discover the landmarks that define the soul of Savoca.

Capuchin Monastery and Catacombs

Delve into the depths of Savoca's history by exploring the Capuchin Monastery and Catacombs. Founded in the 16th century, the monastery provides a glimpse into the austere lives of Capuchin monks. The catacombs beneath the monastery hold a collection of mummified bodies, providing a unique and somewhat eerie perspective on the town's religious practices.

Santa Lucia Monastery

Perched atop Savoca with a commanding presence, the Santa Lucia Monastery exudes a sense of tranquillity and historical significance. Dating back to the 15th century, this monastery boasts a stunning courtyard and a chapel adorned with frescoes depicting the life of Saint Lucy.

Bar Vitelli

Bar Vitelli is a charming establishment that holds a unique place in cinematic history. Featured prominently in Francis Ford Coppola's iconic film, 'The Godfather', this quaint bar has become a pilgrimage site for movie enthusiasts. With its timeless wooden interiors and vintage decor, visitors can immerse themselves in the nostalgia of the 1970s while enjoying a refreshing drink. Bar Vitelli serves not only as a cinematic landmark but also as a living testament to the enduring appeal of Savoca.

Savoca Archaeological Park

For those with an affinity for ancient history, the Savoca Archaeological Park is a treasure trove of archaeological wonders. Discover remnants of ancient civilizations, including Hellenistic and Roman structures. The park offers a glimpse into Savoca's pre-medieval past, with excavations revealing the layers of historical settlements that once thrived in this Sicilian landscape.

Savoca War Memorial

The Savoca War Memorial is a poignant landmark honouring the town's residents who sacrificed their lives during World War I and II. Set against a backdrop of olive trees, this memorial is a sombre yet important site that pays tribute to the resilience and courage of Savoca's community in the face of historical challenges.

Chiesa di San Michele
The Chiesa di San Michele, a historic church dating back to the 13th century, stands as an architectural marvel and spiritual anchor for Savoca. Adorned with intricate frescoes and Baroque embellishments, this church captivates visitors with its artistic grandeur. The panoramic view from the church square adds to the experience, offering breath-taking vistas of the Ionian Sea and the surrounding countryside.

Piazza Fossia

Piazza Fossia stands at the heart of Savoca, a charming square surrounded by historic buildings and local businesses. This bustling hub is a perfect spot to soak in the town's atmosphere, whether enjoying a leisurely coffee, shopping for local crafts, or simply savouring the ambiance.

Savoca Medieval Aqueduct

The Savoca Medieval Aqueduct is an engineering marvel that whispers of the town's medieval ingenuity. Dating back to the 15th century, this aqueduct served as a vital water supply system for Savoca. Its arches and channels, gracefully traversing the landscape, are a testament to the engineering prowess of the past and offer a scenic backdrop for those exploring the town on foot.

Palazzo Corvaja

Palazzo Corvaja, a noble residence with origins dating back to the 10th century, is a testament to the enduring architectural legacy of Savoca. With its distinctive Norman-Arab influences, this palace is adorned with intricate stonework and elegant balconies. Today, it serves as a cultural centre, hosting events and exhibitions that celebrate the town's artistic and historical heritage.

Savoca Town Hall

The Savoca Town Hall, located in the heart of the town, is a neoclassical building that reflects the administrative hub of Savoca. With its elegant facade and prominent position on Piazza Fossia, the Town Hall is not only a practical centre for civic affairs but also an architectural gem that contributes to the town's visual allure.

Savoca Castle Ruins

Perched atop a hill, the Savoca Castle Ruins command attention with their dramatic silhouette against the Sicilian sky. Although the castle stands in picturesque ruins today, it once played a strategic role in the region's medieval defence. Visitors can wander through the remnants, enjoying panoramic views of the surrounding landscapes and imagining the castle's historical significance.

Embark on a journey through Savoca's landmarks, where each site tells a story of Sicilian history, cultural richness and cinematic allure. From ancient ruins to Baroque palaces, the town unfolds as a living tapestry of the past, inviting visitors to explore its diverse and captivating points of interest.

Flavours of Sicily: Sampling Savoca's culinary treasures

Savoca, a Sicilian jewel embraced by rolling hills and cinematic allure, not only captivates with its historic charm but also entices the palate with a symphony of culinary delights. Each cobblestone street and quaint trattoria in this picturesque town tells a story through its flavours, drawing on Sicily's rich gastronomic heritage. Join us on a gastronomic journey through Savoca, where each culinary delight is a testament to the town's cultural tapestry and the centuries of Sicilian culinary craftsmanship.

Caponata

Savour the Sicilian flavours with Caponata, a vibrant and savoury eggplant-based dish that mirrors the sun-soaked landscapes of the region. Combining eggplants, tomatoes, olives and capers, all harmoniously bathed in a sweet and tangy agrodolce sauce, Caponata exemplifies the art of Sicilian antipasti.

Cassata Siciliana

For those with a sweet tooth, Cassata Siciliana is a Sicilian dessert that beckons indulgence. Layers of sponge cake are soaked in liqueur and stacked with sweetened ricotta, candied fruit and marzipan. The entire creation is then coated in vibrant green icing, creating a visual masterpiece that mirrors the colourful landscapes of Sicily. Cassata Siciliana is a sweet ode to the island's rich culinary traditions.

Arancini di Riso

Embark on a culinary adventure with Savoca's exquisite Arancini di Riso. These golden orbs of joy are crafted from saffron-infused rice, enveloping a heart of flavourful ragù, peas and molten mozzarella. Deep-fried to a crispy perfection, Arancini di Riso showcase the mastery of Sicilian rice dishes, offering a delectable blend of textures and tastes that embody the essence of street food indulgence in Savoca.

Granita al Limone

Beat the Sicilian heat with the refreshing Granita al Limone, a Sicilian lemon granita that captures the zesty essence of the region. Finely crushed ice meets freshly squeezed lemon juice, resulting in a thirst-quenching treat that epitomizes the simplicity and purity of Sicilian flavours. Served in local cafes, Granita al Limone offers a delightful respite and a sensory journey through the citrus groves of Savoca.

Gelato Siciliano

Treat yourself to Gelato Siciliano, a frozen delight that mirrors the abundance of fresh fruits and flavours in Sicily. Whether it's the intense pistachio, fragrant citrus, or velvety chocolate, Savoca's gelato shops offer a sensory journey through Sicily's diverse landscapes.

Sfincione

Delight in the savoury flavours of Sfincione, a Sicilian-style pizza that boasts a thick, fluffy crust and a generous topping of tomatoes, onions, anchovies and a sprinkle of breadcrumbs. Often enjoyed during festive occasions, Sfincione showcases the rustic charm of Sicilian Street food, inviting locals and visitors alike to relish the hearty goodness of this delectable pizza variation.

Sicilian Cannoli

Savour the iconic Sicilian dessert of Cannoli, a delicacy that combines crisp pastry tubes with a luscious ricotta-based filling. Savoca's Cannoli are a testament to the island's pastry mastery, featuring a crunchy shell adorned with pistachios or candied fruit. Each bite unveils a symphony of textures and flavours, making Cannoli an irresistible treat that encapsulates the sweet soul of Savoca.

Pesce Spada alla Ghiotta

Explore the coastal influence in Savoca's cuisine with Pesce Spada alla Ghiotta, a flavourful swordfish dish that captures the essence of the Mediterranean. Grilled to perfection and adorned with a sauce of tomatoes, olives, capers and fresh herbs, this seafood delight showcases Savoca's connection to the bounties of the sea and the vibrant flavours that define Sicilian coastal cuisine.

Insalata di Arance e Finocchi

Refresh your palate with Insalata di Arance e Finocchi, a vibrant salad that celebrates the citrus abundance of Sicily. Sliced oranges mingle with crisp fennel, creating a refreshing and invigorating dish. Dressed with a drizzle of local olive oil and a sprinkle of Sicillian sea salt, this salad captures the essence of Savoca's commitment to fresh and seasonal ingredients.

Ricotta Calda con Miele

Savour a simple yet sublime dessert with Ricotta Calda con Miele, warm ricotta drizzled with golden Sicilian honey. The velvety ricotta, often sourced from local farms, takes on a delicate sweetness when paired with the rich and floral notes of Sicilian honey.

Pasta alla Norma

Indulge in the classic Sicilian comfort food of Pasta alla Norma, a dish inspired by the opera 'Norma' by Vincenzo Bellini. This pasta masterpiece features tubular pasta tossed with a rich tomato sauce, succulent eggplant cubes and a generous sprinkle of ricotta salata. The medley of flavours, ranging from sweet tomato to smoky eggplant, creates a culinary symphony.

Embark on a culinary journey through Savoca, where each delightful dish is a celebration of Sicilian flavours, cultural heritage and the artistry that defines this picturesque town.

Mysteries of Sicily: Exploring Savoca's hidden wonders

Beyond the well-trodden paths and celebrated landmarks, Savoca unveils a treasure trove of hidden gems that add an enchanting layer to its historic charm. These hidden wonders, often known only to locals or the most curious of travellers, beckon those willing to explore the quieter corners of this Sicilian gem. Join us on a journey to discover Savoca's hidden gems, where each secret spot holds a story and contributes to the town's mystique, creating an immersive experience for those seeking the road less travelled.

Grotta di Santa Maria delle Grazie

Tucked away in the hills surrounding Savoca, the Grotta di Santa Maria delle Grazie is a hidden cave chapel that whispers of devotion and serenity. Carved into the rock, this humble sanctuary invites visitors to step into a sacred space adorned with religious artifacts and flickering candles. The Grotta di Santa Maria delle Grazie offers a tranquil retreat from the bustling streets, providing a moment of reflection in the midst of nature's embrace.

Ancient Water Mills

Veiled by the lush foliage along the San Francesco River, the ancient water mills of Savoca are a testament to the town's industrial past. These hidden gems, with their weathered stones and moss-covered wheels, transport visitors to a bygone era. Tucked away from the main thoroughfares, the rhythmic sound of water flowing through these mills provides a soothing soundtrack to the exploration of this hidden corner of Savoca.

Via dell'Arte

Venture off the beaten path and discover Via dell'Arte, a hidden alleyway adorned with vibrant murals and street art. This secret gallery captures the creative spirit of Savoca, offering a visual feast that blends contemporary expression with the town's historical backdrop. Each mural tells a story, adding a modern twist to the narrative of Savoca's artistic identity.

The Secret Garden of San Rocco Church

Behind the walls of San Rocco Church lies a secret garden, a verdant oasis hidden from the eyes of passers-by. This secluded haven, with its fragrant blooms and quiet corners, invites visitors to escape the hustle and bustle of the town. The Secret Garden of San Rocco is a hidden gem that offers a serene retreat, allowing guests to connect with nature in the heart of Savoca.

Sicilian Puppet Theatre Museum

Hidden within the historic walls of Savoca, the Sicilian Puppet Theatre Museum is a cultural gem that showcases the town's connection to the traditional art of marionette theatre. The museum's collection of intricately crafted puppets and vibrant backdrops provides a glimpse into Sicily's rich puppetry heritage. Tucked away from the bustling streets, this hidden museum is a tribute to the storytelling traditions that have enchanted generations.

Vicoletto dell'Amore

Nestled within the labyrinthine streets of Savoca, the Vicoletto dell'Amore is a hidden alley that carries whispers of romantic tales. Adorned with flowering vines and charming doorways, this secluded passageway exudes an air of intimacy. Whether enjoyed as a quiet stroll or a moment of shared connection, the Vicoletto dell'Amore unveils a hidden facet of Savoca's romantic allure.

Fontana Vecchia

In a secluded corner of Savoca stands the Fontana Vecchia, a hidden fountain that once quenched the thirst of locals. This centuries-old gem, tucked away from the main squares, features a worn but dignified facade. Its trickling waters and moss-covered stones offer a glimpse into the historic significance of water sources in Sicilian towns, making Fontana Vecchia a hidden oasis with a story to tell.

Embark on a discovery of Savoca's hidden gems, where each secret spot adds a layer of mystery and allure to this timeless Sicilian town. Beyond the well-known attractions, these hidden wonders invite you to uncover the nuanced stories and unexpected beauty that make Savoca a destination of endless fascination.

Nature's nook: Outdoor adventures amidst Savoca's scenic beauty

Savoca, with its sun-kissed landscapes and historic allure, invites outdoor enthusiasts to embark on a journey of exploration and adventure. Beyond its cobblestone streets and ancient monuments, Savoca unfolds as a haven for outdoor activities, offering a harmonious blend of nature and culture. From panoramic hikes to leisurely bike rides, the town and its surroundings beckon those seeking an active escape. Join us on a discovery of outdoor activities in Savoca, where each adventure unveils a different facet of this Sicilian gem, surrounded by the beauty of the Ionian Sea and rolling hills.

Hiking to Capo Sant'Alessio

Embark on a scenic hiking adventure to Capo Sant'Alessio, a promontory that graces Savoca's coastline. The trail, surrounded by the fragrant Mediterranean flora, offers breath-taking views of the Ionian Sea and the surrounding landscapes. As you ascend, the historic charm of Savoca unfolds below, creating a perfect fusion of nature and culture. The hike culminates in panoramic vistas that reward your efforts, making Capo Sant'Alessio a must-visit for hiking enthusiasts.

Cycling through lemon groves

Explore the picturesque countryside of Savoca on two wheels, pedalling through lush lemon groves and charming villages. The town's outskirts provide a network of cycling routes that wind through fragrant orchards and offer glimpses of rural Sicilian life. The gentle terrain makes cycling accessible for all skill levels, creating an immersive and leisurely experience as you soak in the beauty of Savoca's agricultural landscapes.

Bird watching along the San Francesco river

For nature enthusiasts and bird watchers, the banks of the San Francesco River provide an idyllic setting to observe local avian residents. Stroll along the riverside paths, where the tranquil flow of water and the surrounding greenery create a peaceful habitat for a variety of bird species. Bring your binoculars and camera to capture the diverse birdlife that calls this Sicillian river home.

Picnicking in the secret garden

Escape the urban hustle and indulge in a leisurely picnic in the Secret Garden of San Rocco Church. This hidden oasis, with its fragrant blooms and shaded corners, offers a perfect setting for a relaxed outdoor meal. Pack a basket with Sicilian delights, enjoy the gentle breeze and let the tranquil ambiance of the Secret Garden enhance your outdoor dining experience.

Rock climbing at Santuario di Madonna delle Grazie

For those seeking a more adventurous outdoor pursuit, the cliffs surrounding the Santuario di Madonna delle Grazie offer opportunities for rock climbing. The limestone formations and panoramic views make this a unique climbing spot in the Savoca region. Whether you're a seasoned climber or a beginner looking for a new challenge, the crags around the sanctuary provide a thrilling outdoor experience.

Yoga retreats in the countryside

Reconnect with mind and body amidst the serene landscapes of Savoca with yoga retreats offered in the countryside. Local instructors curate immersive experiences that combine yoga and meditation, taking advantage of the tranquil surroundings to enhance relaxation and mindfulness. Join a retreat to experience the harmonious synergy of Sicilian nature and the practice of yoga.

Horseback riding through vineyards

Discover the charm of Savoca's countryside on horseback, riding through vineyards and rolling hills. Guided horseback tours offer a unique perspective on the town's agricultural heritage and panoramic vistas. Whether you're a seasoned rider or a novice, the equestrian trails around Savoca provide an enchanting outdoor experience in the company of gentle and well-trained horses.

Sailing along the Ionian Coast

For water enthusiasts, set sail along the Ionian coast to experience the beauty of Savoca from the sea. Charter a boat or join a sailing tour to explore hidden coves, coastal cliffs and pristine beaches. The gentle sea breeze and panoramic views of Savoca's coastline create an unforgettable sailing experience with the town's historic charm in the backdrop.

Outdoor photography expeditions

Capture the essence of Savoca's beauty through outdoor photography expeditions. Join local photographers or embark on a self-guided exploration to frame the town's historic architecture, scenic landscapes and vibrant street life. The ever-changing light and shadow patterns create a captivating canvas for photography enthusiasts to document the timeless allure of Savoca.

Stargazing in the Sicilian night sky
As the sun sets over Savoca, embrace the enchantment of the night sky with stargazing excursions. Far from city lights, the town's surroundings offer clear views of celestial wonders. Join astronomy experts or simply find a quiet spot to gaze at the stars, connecting with the vast universe above in the peaceful embrace of Savoca.

Unveil the outdoor wonders of Savoca, where each activity immerses you in the natural beauty and cultural richness of this Sicilian treasure. From adrenaline-pumping adventures to serene nature walks, Savoca invites you to explore its outdoor offerings and create lasting memories in the heart of the Mediterranean.

Festive flourish: Embracing the cultural heritage of Savoca

Savoca, steeped in history and vibrant cultural heritage, comes alive with a tapestry of local traditions and festivals that celebrate Sicilian identity. From religious processions to lively celebrations, each event in Savoca reflects the town's deep connection to its roots. Join us on a journey through the traditions and festivals of Savoca, where the streets echo with the melodies of folklore, the aromas of traditional cuisine and the vibrant colours of local festivities. These cultural expressions offer a unique glimpse into the heart and soul of this charming Sicilian town.

Festa di San Michele (September)

The Festa di San Michele, dedicated to the town's patron saint, Saint Michael, is a cherished religious celebration that takes place on September 29th. The festivities commence with a solemn religious procession, where the statue of San Michele is carried through the streets of Savoca. Pilgrims and locals join in the procession, adorned in traditional attire, creating a vibrant spectacle that reflects the deep devotion of the community.

Easter Week Celebrations (March - April)

Easter Week in Savoca is marked by a series of religious and cultural events that capture the essence of Sicilian traditions. The Holy Week processions, particularly on Good Friday, feature solemn parades carrying statues depicting scenes from the Passion of Christ. Locals participate in these processions and the streets are adorned with intricate religious decorations.

Sagra del Marrone (October)

As autumn colours paint the landscape, Savoca hosts the Sagra del Marrone, a lively Chestnut Festival that celebrates the harvest season. This festival highlights the significance of chestnuts in Sicilian cuisine and culture. Visitors can indulge in roasted chestnuts, chestnut-based dishes and traditional Sicilian sweets. The festival also features live music, dancing and local artisans showcasing their crafts, creating a festive atmosphere that brings the community and visitors together.

Festa di Sant'Anna (July)

The Festa di Sant'Anna, dedicated to Saint Anne, is a summertime celebration that unfolds with religious devotion and communal joy. The festival includes a procession featuring the statue of Sant'Anna adorned with flowers. Pilgrims and locals gather to participate in the religious events, followed by traditional music, dance and a lively fair. The Festa di Sant'Anna encapsulates the Sicilian spirit of combining reverence with festivity, creating an atmosphere of unity and cultural pride.

Processione dei Misteri (March/April)

On Good Friday, Savoca is enveloped in a profound religious atmosphere during the Processione dei Misteri. This solemn procession commemorates the Stations of the Cross and the Passion of Christ. Elaborate wooden sculptures, depicting scenes from the crucifixion, are carried through the streets with profound reverence. The townspeople, dressed in black, participate in this moving event, creating a poignant ambiance that reflects the spiritual depth of the community.

Carnival Celebrations (February)

Savoca embraces the festive spirit of Carnival with colourful celebrations, lively parades and traditional masks. During Carnival season, the streets come alive with music, dance and the playful energy of locals and visitors alike. The Carnival festivities in Savoca provide a platform for creativity and expression, with elaborate costumes, theatrical performances and the joyous tradition of the 'Carnevale di Cori' (Carnival of Chorus), where groups perform satirical songs in the local dialect.

Sagra del Pesce Spada (August)

Celebrating Savoca's coastal heritage, the Sagra del Pesce Spada is a festival dedicated to the renowned Sicilian swordfish. Typically held in the summer, this culinary event showcases the skills of local fishermen and chefs in preparing the iconic swordfish dishes. Visitors can savour grilled swordfish, pasta with swordfish and other seafood delights while enjoying live music and entertainment.

Infiorata di Savoca (May/June)

Infiorata di Savoca is an enchanting flower festival that transforms the town's streets into vibrant tapestries of colour. Taking place in May, local artists and residents create intricate floral carpets along the main thoroughfares, depicting religious motifs, intricate patterns and vivid scenes. The festival is a visual feast that combines artistry with natural beauty.

Festival of Santa Lucia (December)

In honour of the patron saint of sight, Santa Lucia, Savoca hosts a festival that combines religious reverence with cultural festivities. The celebration includes a procession featuring the statue of Santa Lucia adorned with candles. Locals pay homage to the saint and the event is followed by traditional Sicilian music, dance and a festive fair.

Festa della Vendemmia (September)

As the vineyards around Savoca come alive with the bounty of the grape harvest, the town celebrates the Festa della Vendemmia. This joyful festival, held in September, pays homage to the town's winemaking heritage. Visitors can participate in grape stomping, taste local wines and enjoy traditional Sicilian music and dance.

Living Nativity Scene (December)

During the Christmas season, Savoca hosts a Living Nativity Scene that re-enacts the biblical story of the birth of Jesus. Locals, dressed in period costumes, portray characters from the nativity narrative, creating a serene and contemplative atmosphere. The Living Nativity Scene is a cultural tradition that invites both residents and visitors to experience the spirit of Christmas in a unique and meaningful way.

Immerse yourself in the vibrant traditions and festivals of Savoca, where each celebration is a testament to the town's cultural richness, community spirit and deep-rooted connections to Sicilian heritage.

Cultural compass: Savoca's travel tips for discerning explorers

Stepping into the timeless embrace of Savoca is like discovering a hidden Sicilian gem, where historic charm and breath-taking landscapes converge. To ensure an enriching and seamless experience in this picturesque town, it's wise to heed a few travel tips that unveil the best of Savoca's offerings. From navigating the historic streets to savouring local cuisine, these tips serve as a compass for travellers eager to immerse themselves in the cultural tapestry of Savoca. Join us as we unravel essential travel insights to make your journey through this Sicilian haven all the more memorable.

Exploring on Foot

Savoca's narrow streets and historical sites are best explored on foot. The town's medieval layout, adorned with cobblestone alleys and ancient archways, invites leisurely strolls. Comfortable footwear is advisable, allowing you to wander through the charming squares, discover hidden corners and ascend to panoramic viewpoints.

Visit Off-Peak for Tranquillity

To experience Savoca in all its tranquillity and avoid crowds, consider visiting during the off-peak seasons, typically in the spring (April to June) or fall (September to October). The weather during these periods is pleasant and you'll have the opportunity to engage with the locals without the bustling atmosphere of peak tourist times. Off-peak visits provide a more intimate experience, allowing you to appreciate Savoca's authenticity at your own pace.

Respect Local Traditions

Savoca takes great pride in its local traditions and festivals. If your visit coincides with one of these events, embrace the opportunity to participate and witness the vibrant cultural expressions of the town. Whether it's a religious procession or a lively festival, respecting and appreciating these traditions fosters a deeper connection with the community and enriches your overall experience.

Learn Basic Italian Phrases

While many locals in Savoca may understand and speak some English, learning a few basic Italian phrases can enhance your interactions and make your experience more enjoyable. The effort to communicate in the local language is often appreciated and can lead to more authentic encounters with the residents.

Cash and Cards

While major establishments may accept credit cards, it's advisable to carry some cash, especially when exploring smaller shops or enjoying street food. Inform your bank of your travel dates to avoid any issues with card transactions and have some euros on hand for a seamless experience.

Stay Hydrated and Sun-Protected

Savoca's Mediterranean climate can be warm, especially in the summer months. Ensure you stay hydrated by carrying a water bottle and protect yourself from the sun with sunscreen, a hat and sunglasses, particularly if you plan to spend extended periods outdoors.

Following these travel tips will not only enhance your journey through Savoca but also allow you to connect with the town's essence in a more meaningful way. Whether you're an avid explorer or a leisurely wanderer, these insights ensure that every moment in Savoca becomes a cherished part of your Sicilian adventure.

Echoes of elegance: Wrapping up the Savoca sojourn with cultural reveries

As you carry the essence of Savoca beyond its stone walls, may the echoes of its cultural symphony resonate in your travels. The medieval architecture, the timeless landscapes and the warmth of Savoca's people become companions on your journey through Sicily.

The closing thoughts on Savoca are not merely an end but a continuation-a continuation of the stories told by cobblestone streets, the melodies played by ancient churches and the cinematic dreams woven into the fabric of this Sicilian village.Farewell to Savoca-a Sicilian reverie that lingers as a cherished melody in the heart of your Mediterranean odyssey.

Farewell to Italy's Hidden Treasures: Reflecting on Our Journey

As we draw the curtains on this captivating journey through Italy's hidden gems, it's time to reflect on the myriad experiences, sights and sensations that have enriched our exploration of this remarkable country. From the sun-kissed shores of Sorrento to the historic streets of Varenna, from the medieval charm of Savoca to the breath-taking vistas of Ravello, each destination has left an indelible mark on our hearts and minds. Throughout our journey, we've uncovered the layers of Italy's rich tapestry, delving into its storied past, vibrant culture and timeless beauty. From ancient ruins to medieval castles, from bustling piazzas to tranquil vineyards, Italy's landscapes are steeped in history and alive with the echoes of generations past.

No exploration of Italy would be complete without indulging in its delectable culinary delights. From the tangy taste of Limoncello in Sorrento to the savoury flavours of seafood risotto in Cinque Terre, each dish tells a story of tradition, innovation and passion. As we bid farewell to the mouth-watering flavours of Italy, let us carry with us the memories of shared meals, lively conversations and unforgettable gastronomic experiences.

From hidden alleyways to panoramic viewpoints, from ancient ruins to pristine beaches, Italy's hidden gems have offered us a treasure trove of discoveries waiting to be uncovered. As we bid adieu to these lesser-known destinations, let us cherish the moments of wonder and awe that have filled our hearts with joy and our minds with inspiration.

But fear not, dear readers, for our adventure is far from over. In the next instalment of this eBook, we'll venture even further off the beaten path, uncovering 10-11 additional destinations that promise to captivate our imaginations and stir our souls. From the majestic beauty of the Dolomites to the ancient ruins of Pompeii, from the enchanting canals of Venice to the rugged coastline of Puglia, our journey continues to unfold with new adventures, new discoveries and new memories waiting to be made. So, stay tuned, dear travellers and prepare to embark on another unforgettable journey through Italy's hidden treasures. Until then, arrivederci e a presto!

Setting the Stage for Italy's Continued Adventure

As we reluctantly bid arrivederci to the enchanting destinations we've explored thus far, a sense of both satisfaction and anticipation fills the air. From the timeless allure of Pitigliano to the serene beauty of Tellaro, each stop on our journey has offered a glimpse into the rich tapestry of Italy's hidden treasures. But as we close this chapter, a new adventure beckons—one that promises to transport us even further into the heart and soul of this captivating country.

Picture yourself standing on the cobbled streets of an ancient village, surrounded by centuries-old buildings steeped in history. You can almost taste the aroma of freshly baked bread wafting from a nearby trattoria, hear the distant strains of music echoing through the narrow alleyways and feel the warmth of the Mediterranean sun on your skin. This is Italy, a land of endless wonders and undiscovered delights, waiting to be explored.

In the second part of our eBook, we'll delve deeper into Italy's hidden gems, uncovering 10-11 additional destinations that promise to ignite your imagination and awaken your sense of adventure. From the majestic peaks of the Dolomites to the sun-drenched shores of Sicily, from the bustling markets of Naples to the tranquil vineyards of Piedmont, each destination offers its own unique blend of beauty, culture and charm.

But it's not just the destinations themselves that will captivate you—it's the journey. Imagine embarking on a road trip through the rolling hills of Tuscany, stopping to sample local wines at family-owned vineyards along the way. Picture yourself cruising along the Amalfi Coast, winding your way through picturesque villages perched on cliffs high above the sparkling sea. Envision exploring ancient ruins that whisper tales of empires long past, wandering through labyrinthine streets that lead to hidden courtyards and secret gardens.

As we prepare to set out on this new adventure, let anticipation fill your heart and excitement guide your steps. The wonders of Italy await, dear readers and together, we'll discover them all. So, pack your bags, grab your passport and get ready to embark on another unforgettable journey through Italy's hidden treasures. Until then, let your imagination soar and your wanderlust thrive. The best is yet to come.

About the author

JAY CHANDARANA - As an avid explorer and passionate advocate for discovering the lesser-known corners of our world, I am dedicated to embarking on journeys that unravel the mysteries of unexplored destinations. While my travels may not always take me to the most popular tourist spots, my fervor for unearthing hidden gems and sharing them with fellow adventurers is unparalleled.

Despite not having personally visited every place documented in my works, my passion for exploration knows no bounds. Each journey I undertake is meticulously researched, drawing from a wealth of resources, local insights, and firsthand accounts to provide readers with authentic experiences.

My commitment to uncovering the allure of undiscovered locales stems from a desire to transcend conventional travel narratives. Through my writing, I aim to shed light on the richness and diversity of lesser-explored regions, inviting readers to venture beyond the beaten path and immerse themselves in the cultural tapestry of our world.

While renowned destinations certainly hold their allure, I firmly believe that true discovery lies in the exploration of the unfamiliar. It is my mission to inspire others to step off the well-trodden trail and embark on their own adventures, forging connections with places and people they never knew existed.

Join me on a journey of exploration and discovery, as we traverse landscapes both familiar and foreign, uncovering the hidden treasures that await us off the beaten path. Together, let us embark on a quest to broaden our horizons, enrich our perspectives, and ignite a passion for discovery that knows no bounds

Stay connected beyond the pages – join the journey on social media

YouTube: https://www.youtube.com/@incognitodestinations
Instagram: https://www.instagram.com/incognitodestinations
Amazon Catalog: https://amazon.com/author/jaychandarana
Apple books: https://books.apple.com/us/book/revelations-in-the-soul-of-italy/id6479964311?ls=1